MW01616872

Shabbat.
A Day
to Create
Yourself.

Building Character, Shaping Perspectives and Finding Happiness through Shabbat.

Rabbi Warren Goldstein

A Day to Create Yourself is written with intellect and heart, and overflows with foundational religious and philosophical principles, from which all readers will derive great benefit. The book lays out the foundations of the holy Shabbos in relevant and practical terms.

Our sages tell us that Shabbos is the 'soulmate' of the Jewish people. Every match has a matchmaker, and there are certain people who are blessed to be matchmakers who set up the Jewish people with their soulmate, the holy Shabbos. Rabbi Goldstein has merited to match many Jews with their Creator, our Father in Heaven, and to bring awareness of this hidden treasure, the precious gift of Shabbos, which the Holy One Blessed is He has given to us. The merit of his spreading Shabbos observance across the entire globe is immeasurable and indescribable. Those who have already merited to taste the life-giving sustenance of Shabbos will relight its fire by reading his illuminating words in this book. Furthermore, even those who have not yet merited to see its light, through reading this relevant and practical book, will, by the grace of Hashem, merit to be reunited with Shabbos.

- Rabbi Shmuel Kamenetsky, Rosh Yeshiva of the Talmudical Yeshiva of Philadelphia

A Day to Create Yourself reveals the secrets, the inner dimensions, of Shabbat, and brings to light not just their meaning, but their application. Rabbi Goldstein adopts a completely unique approach to this subject, contemplating the powerful impact of Shabbat on the individual, and how, in keeping Shabbat, a person can form an intimate understanding of it and an emotional attachment to it.

I have no doubt this book will strengthen the Covenant between the Jewish people and the Creator.

- Rabbi David Lau, Chief Rabbi of Israel

I was moved to tears while reading sections of *A Day to Create Yourself*. Not only does Rabbi Goldstein explain the meaning of Shabbos, in terms of Jewish law and thought, he also explains the meaning of the big picture of Judaism as a whole, the foundations of our worldview.

- Rabbi Hershel Schachter, Rosh Yeshiva and Rosh Kollel of RIETS

A Day to Create Yourself covers Shabbat from every possible angle. I was amazed to see how, in the book, all the various facets of Shabbat converge into this all-encompassing theme of self-creation - and how every Shabbat is a chance to create ourselves anew.

- Rabbi Aryeh Stern, Chief Rabbi of Jerusalem

To appreciate and absorb the gift of the Sabbath, one must be knowledgeable about it. The Sabbath speaks to us but we have to wish to listen to it. In *A Day to Create Yourself*, Rabbi Goldstein addresses the issue of knowing, understanding, and observing the Sabbath in all of its ramifications and nuances. This is a book for every Jew no matter what one's personal outlook and beliefs may be. In fact, it is both the primer and encyclopedia of Jewish life, thought, and practice.

- Rabbi Berel Wein, founder of the Destiny Foundation and Rabbi of the Beit Knesset HaNasi in Jerusalem

I was privileged to be in South Africa for the first Shabbos Project, that most sublime Shabbos, which was kept by the vast majority of South African Jewry. With his tremendous abilities and influence, as one who has merited Heavenly assistance, Rabbi Goldstein has succeeded in bringing this concept to thousands of Jewish communities across the globe. And now, he has dedicated a great book, *A Day to Create Yourself*, with ideas and discussions that demonstrate the personal heights each and every one of us can reach by keeping Shabbos.

- Rabbi Osher Weiss, Av Beis Din and Rosh Yeshiva of Darchei Torah

In *A Day to Create Yourself*, the distinguished and illustrious Rabbi Goldstein, a man of sage wisdom, lays out how to build character and find happiness through keeping Shabbat. All the themes have been organized into brief inspirational chapters, and are based on our Holy Torah and the teachings of our sages. He has set out the contents precisely and thoughtfully, golden apples presented in silver showcases.

- Rabbi Yitzchak Yosef, Chief Rabbi of Israel

A Day to Create Yourself beautifully accents the spiritual dimensions of this holy day of rest. It reminds us of the real ways in which Shabbat can elevate our lives and our souls, and shows us why Shabbat is the national treasure of our people. Through the global Shabbat Project, Rabbi Goldstein has brought the Jewish world that much closer together, and now, through this illuminating book, he has given us an important addition to the collective Jewish library.

- President Isaac Herzog, President of the State of Israel

In *A Day to Create Yourself*, Rabbi Goldstein takes us on multiple journeys all at once. The book demonstrates the important and fascinating wisdom of Shabbat; the ways it interacts with and reflects the way we live, and - most important from the perspective of social science - how it guides us to make changes to improve our daily lives. While reading *A Day to Create Yourself*, we don't always know which exact journey we are on, but it is always dynamic and captivating.

- Professor Dan Ariely, James B. Duke Professor of psychology and behavioral economics at Duke University, New York Times best-selling author

Rabbi Goldstein has done extraordinary things so many times in his life. As Chief Rabbi, as the architect of what has become a new global consciousness of Sabbath awareness, and now, as the author of an extraordinary exploration of one of the most well-known observances of the Jewish people, and also one of the most intimate. *A Day to Create Yourself* is an essential for any home dedicated to growing both outward as part of a larger community, and inward as the start of creating peace, wholeness, and holiness every blessed week of the year.

- Mayim Bialik, Emmy-nominated star of The Big Bang Theory, Jeopardy host, neuroscientist

A Day to Create Yourself is Shabbat Project founder Rabbi Dr. Warren Goldstein's latest endeavor to bring Shabbat to the forefront of global Jewish consciousness. With this book, he has mined centuries of classic ideas and commentaries from some of the greatest Sages of the Jewish people - and emerged with something unique and all of his own making. An inspiring read for scholars and novices alike. Deeply philosophical, but not dense. And full of practical insights that will enrich the Shabbat experience of anyone who reads it.

- **Senator Joseph Lieberman,** former US Senator and Vice Presidential Candidate, author of *The Gift of Rest*

A Day to Create Yourself presents an articulate and timely message about the importance of Shabbat as a source of Jewish unity, courage, and strength, and of our solidarity and pride as a nation. This is something I've personally experienced through the various stages of my public and personal life in service of the Jewish people, and have witnessed through Rabbi Goldstein's work on The Shabbat Project. I welcome this book.

- **Natan Sharansky,** former Israeli Deputy Prime Minister and head of the Jewish Agency

This book is dedicated in honor of

ERIC SAMSON of blessed memory,
and his beloved SHEILA, may she be well,

and in honor of

JOHN HILLEL MOSHAL of blessed memory,
and his beloved ANNA, may she be well.

The patriarchs and matriarchs of two of the great Jewish philanthropic families of our time, pillars of support to the South African Jewish community, the State of Israel and the Jewish world, families who, with vision and boundless generosity, make this world a better place, and who I am honored to call my partners and friends.

אָמַר לוֹ הקב״ה לְמֹשֶׁה: מַתָּנָה טוֹבָה יֵשׁ לִי בְּבֵית גְּנָזַי - וְשַׁבָּת שְׁמָהּ.

God said to Moses, "I have a precious gift in My treasure house and its name is Shabbat."

- Talmud Shabbat 10b

Dear reader,

Writing this book has been an eye-opening experience for me. As I delved into our sources, I caught a glimpse of the deeper meaning of these words of the Talmud.

I learned that the Divine gift of Shabbat goes beyond the simple kindness of God granting us a day of complete rest from the demands of daily life - although that gift cannot be underestimated, especially in today's frenzied times.

I discovered a bigger, grander idea - the ultimate gift of Shabbat is that God has given us a day to create the best version of ourselves, our family, and our world; to build our character and cultivate the vital traits we need to thrive; to shape our perspectives with His illuminating wisdom; to learn and experience a Divine recipe for lasting happiness.

Thank you for giving this book your time and attention. I hope that doing so will enhance your enjoyment and appreciation - as much as it did for me in writing it - of the precious gift delivered to us with Divine love at sunset every Friday.

Warren Feldst

CONTENTS

FOUNDATIONS

1 A Day to Create Yourself

The secret to uncovering the essence of Shabbat begins with how we define work, productivity – and creativity.

To survive and thrive in the world, we have a lot to do. We work to acquire food, clothing and shelter, to make a living, to build and shape our environment. We are drawn to measure what we have accomplished through our work, evaluating our worth by what we have created. All the things we can touch and count become symbols of our achievements. This is one kind of human creativity.

But there is another kind that produces accomplishments that are not material, tangible or quantifiable, that cannot be weighed or measured or priced, products that cannot be seen or touched. This is the work of becoming a better person – a person of values and meaning, of character and wisdom, with rich and enduring relationships, dedicated to a life of doing good.

These two kinds of work and creativity are inextricably bound up with human identity. We need both. We need to build and shape the physical world around us and we need to build and shape our inner world. How do we balance the two? How do we find the space and time to engage in two such profoundly different modes of creative work?

Shabbat is the answer. It gives Divine rhythm and balance to our lives. "Six days you shall work and accomplish all your tasks."[1] From Sunday to Friday, we work to create our material world. "And the seventh day is Shabbat, for God."[2] Shabbat is the day for a special kind of work. We focus exclusively on creating ourselves; on the inner world of character and relationships. Of course, during the week, too, there are continual opportunities to grow spiritually through all of our other mitzvahs. But on Shabbat this inner creativity is our sole focus.

Just like God, the ultimate Creator, we too are creators. To create is deeply embedded in our souls, which are a reflection of the Divine.[3] We have a mitzvah to emulate God, which refers to His compassion and kindness,[4] but also His creativity.[5] We follow in God's footsteps, living in the very same cycle with which He created the world.[6] He created the physical universe for six days, and on the seventh He created Shabbat. The seventh day was an essential part of Creation.[7] A completely different dimension of it. The spiritual dimension. Just like God, for six days we create our physical world, and on the seventh we create the spiritual world. And it's not just that we live as a shadow in God's cycle of creativity – we are His "partners in creation,"[8] active participants in His constant renewal and creation of our world.

On Shabbat we stop creating the physical world, we cease imposing our will on our environment,[9] and we turn our creative partnership with God inwards. We create ourselves and our relationships. God gave us the laws of nature as our partner for creating the physical world during the week. And He gave us Shabbat as our partner for creating ourselves and our inner world.[10]

The immersive experience of Shabbat gives us the framework, space and guidance to create ourselves. It gives us the wisdom to be successful in this great endeavor. It brings balance to our lives. It reminds us that we cannot only be creators and shapers of the physical world *out there*; that once a week, we need to pause and focus our creative energy inwards. When we cease all *external* creative work, we can focus instead on *internal* creative work – on developing ourselves and our most precious relationships. And through this process of self-creation, Shabbat rewards us with a Divine recipe for finding happiness.

Shabbat reminds us that our purpose goes beyond mere physical survival; that we have a higher calling – to become great people. Of course, both physical and spiritual creation are essential. This is the rhythm God has given our lives: six days for creating the world, and then one day for bringing it all home – creating ourselves.

Shabbat reminds us that our most important accomplishments in life cannot be touched or measured or priced – that our greatest work of creation is ourselves.

Chapter Notes

[1] Exodus 20:9

[2] Exodus 20:10

[3] See Rabbeinu Bechaye, Genesis 25:8.

[4] Deuteronomy 10:12, 11:22, 13:5, 28:9, Talmud, Sota 14a; Talmud, Shabbat 133b; Rambam, Sefer HaMitzvot, Positive Mitzvah 8; Rambam, Mishne Torah, Hilchot Deot 1:5-6; Sefer HaChinuch, mitzvah 611

[5] Rabbi Yosef Dov Soloveitchik, Halachic Man 2:1; see also Rabbi Moshe Cordovero, Ramak, Tomer Devora, which is dedicated entirely to the topic of emulating God in all of His attributes, which serve as a model for our character traits.

[6] This relationship between Shabbat and the attainment of Godliness is explained by Rabbi Avraham Grodzinski, Torat Avraham, Shabbat V'Aliya 3.

[7] See Chapter 38 below.

[8] Talmud, Shabbat 119b; see Chapter 29 below.

[9] Rabbi S.R. Hirsch Genesis 2:1-3, Exodus 20:8-11, Deuteronomy 5:12-15 and Horeb on the mitzvah of Shabbat

[10] The ideas in this paragraph are based on Rabbi Yaakov Tzvi Mecklenburg, HaKetav VeHaKabbala, Exodus 20:10, as he explains the Midrash, Bereishit Rabba 11:8.

2 | Character, Perspectives, and Happiness

What does it mean to create ourselves? How do we do it? Where do we even start? And how does Shabbat enable self-creation?

To answer these questions, we must delve into deeper mysteries. Why did God make Shabbat a mitzvah? Why did He define it so specifically in terms of what we do and don't do on Shabbat? Why not, for that matter, leave it up to us to decide how to rest? Why does God want us to keep Shabbat?

These are questions we can never fully answer because to do so would be to know the Mind of the Creator in a way that no human being can. "No man can see Me and live"[1] is what God told Moses, our greatest prophet.[2] As long as the soul is embedded in a body we cannot truly grasp God or His plans, and therefore, as the Talmud teaches us, the deeper Divine intent behind the mitzvahs remains essentially unknowable.[3]

So where does that leave us? Is there anything we can understand about the essence of Shabbat and why we keep it? Should we delve deeper? The answer to all these questions is an emphatic "yes."

In this we turn to the guidance and wisdom of one of the great sages of Jewish history, whose writings we study to this day. Rabbi Moshe ben Nachman, better known as the Ramban, lived in 13th century Gerona and was the leader of Spanish Jewry. An acclaimed commentator on the Chumash and the Talmud, and a master of Kabbalah as well as an accomplished physician, he would later play a pivotal role in reviving the Jewish community in Jerusalem following the Crusades, building a synagogue that still stands today.

The Ramban[4] establishes a philosophy of the mitzvahs based on the Midrash[5] that says that God gave us the mitzvahs to purify and refine us. God does not need us to obey Him for *His* sake and for *His* benefit.[6] The mitzvahs are there for *our* benefit; by doing God's will, we become better, more elevated people.[7] He formulated the mitzvahs as catalyzing transformative experiences that enable us to create ourselves – to realize our own potential and achieve greatness.[8]

Of course, the mitzvahs aren't mere *suggestions* for successful living. On a foundational level, we keep the mitzvahs because God instructs us to.[9] We are not privy to His deeper spiritual reasons for commanding us to carry out these specific actions with all their specific details.[10] Those reasons remain with Him. But, according to the Ramban's philosophy of mitzvahs, part of why God wants us to keep them is because they're good for us and guide us on a path of self-transformation and self-realization – a path of self-creation.

We come into this world on a Divine mission to create ourselves. We are born in a state of pure potential. The greatest creation we create in the course of our lives is ourselves. And to achieve this life purpose, God gave us His mitzvahs as tools to catalyze our personal transformation, to actualize the awesome potential contained in our Godly soul. We are called on to be creators like God, and to partner with Him in creating ourselves.[11]

But self-creation seems a vague term. How do we define it? What does self-transformation look like? What are we striving for?

The Ramban says that through the mitzvahs, we transform ourselves in two areas: character and perspectives. These two parts of ourselves determine everything about us: who we are, how we live and what we do.

Our character traits shape how we respond to situations and people, challenges and opportunities, temptations and insights. Are we humble or arrogant, kind or cruel, gentle or angry, jealous or generous, selfish or idealistic? Our character directs our actions and thoughts and the way we live.

Our perspectives shape how we *see* the world. They shape our ideas and identity, values and principles, philosophy and vision. They shape our life goals and frame our reality. Everything we see and experience is colored by our perspectives – our ideas of what life is all about.

God gives us the mitzvahs to help align our character traits and perspectives with Him. When we fulfill the mitzvahs, we don't just go through the motions. We embark on a Divinely guided process of real personal transformation. God's vision for us is that the commandments become catalysts for creating ourselves by molding us into people of wisdom, humility, generosity, compassion, integrity and so much more; that they guide us to the foundational truths and ideas of existence and of our purpose in this world.

There is another dimension to the mitzvahs, according to the Ramban. They are a Divine formula for living optimally and happily in this world.[12] This idea emerges powerfully from the Torah's call to "live by them"[13] – to become truly alive through fulfilling the commandments, which are the paths to experiencing the ultimate quality of life and living "with joy and with goodness of heart."[14]

This is how it must be, if we consider that before creating the physical universe, God referred to the Torah as His blueprint for creation.[15] He created us with the mitzvahs in mind. Therefore, we function best and thrive – as a society and as individuals – when we are aligned with His blueprint for our world. In this way, the mitzvahs are not only the pathway to eternal reward in the next world, but a formula for living optimally and enjoying life in this world – a recipe for finding happiness right here, right now.

In this book we will explore Shabbat using the conceptual framework of the Ramban's philosophy of mitzvahs. We will reflect on the character traits it nurtures within us and grasp the vast perspectives it affords us – all the while making our lives happier.

[1] Exodus 33:20

[2] Deuteronomy 34:10; Rambam, Mishna, Sanhedrin 10:1, Principle of Faith 7

[3] Talmud, Pesachim 119a; Talmud, Sanhedrin 21b; see also Talmud, Berachot 33b.

[4] Ramban, Deuteronomy 22:6

[5] Midrash, Bereishit Rabba 44:1

[6] Job 35:6-7; Jerusalem Talmud, Nedarim 9:1, cited by the Ramban

[7] Deuteronomy 6:24, 10:13, cited by the Ramban to point out that God, Himself, says that the purpose of mitzvahs is for our benefit.

[8] The Ramban articulates his philosophy of mitzvahs in the context of the mitzvah of *shiluach hakein*, which applies if you approach a bird's nest and want to take the eggs or chicks. The Torah says that you must first send the mother bird away so that she does not see you taking her young. The Ramban says that the mitzvah is designed to instill within us the character trait of compassion, by teaching us to empathize with the feelings of the mother bird and to act to protect her from the pain of separation from her young. Using this mitzvah as the starting point, he formulates his philosophy of mitzvahs as it is explained in the main text above.

[9] Talmud, Berachot 33a-b; Midrash, Mechilta D'Rabbi Yishmael 20:3, cited by the Ramban to teach that we need to be willing to accept the mitzvahs purely as decrees of the King.

[10] Talmud, Nidda 9a and Talmud, Yoma 14a, both based on Ecclesiastes 7:23; Bamidbar Rabba 19:3, based on Ecclesiastes 7:23; Midrash, Kohelet Rabba 7:23, 7:26; Midrash Tanchuma, Chukat 6; see also Ramban, Deuteronomy 22:6, based on Ecclesiastes 7:23. See also Sefer HaChinuch, mitzvot 95, 159, 397, 545.

[11] See Chapter 29 below.

[12] This understanding of the mitzvahs as a formula for living with happiness in this world is based on the approach of Rabbi Yerucham Levovitz, Daat Torah, Bamidbar, Parshat Beha'alotcha, p. 84-86, based on Ibn Ezra and Ramban in their commentaries to Leviticus 18:5. See also Rabbi Yeshayahu HaLevi Horowitz, Shelah, Torah SheBichtav, Mishpatim, Derech Chaim 4.

[13] Leviticus 18:5

Chapter Notes

[14] Deuteronomy 28:47. This is based on Rabbi Levovitz's (ibid.) interpretation of the verse.

[15] Midrash, Bereishit Rabba 1:1; Zohar 2:161a

3 | A Formula to Create Yourself

To understand how Shabbat is a uniquely designed formula for self-creation – in terms of character and perspectives – we first need to understand the concept of a mitzvah and how it works.

Self-creation must, of necessity, be a holistic process. Human beings are complex and multi-faceted. We are spiritual and physical, intellectual and emotional. This unique combination of body and soul means that for any process of personal transformation to be effective, it must engage both.

This idea lies at the heart of the concept of a mitzvah.[1] Literally translated as "commandment," it almost always takes the form of a physical action, which conforms to a very specific formula. The physical, external aspect of a mitzvah operates as a catalyst for the spiritual, internal process of self-creation; for transforming our character and perspectives. These two elements of a mitzvah – internal and external – are intertwined, and interact with each other in a virtuous cycle of self-creation, with external actions catalyzing internal change, which in turn inspires further positive actions.

There are two types of mitzvahs: those we fulfill by *doing*, and those we fulfill by *not doing*; those that command us to act and those that command us not to act.[2] There are actions we do to become better people, and there are actions we refrain from doing in order not to damage our character or skew our perspectives. There are actions that bring out the best in us and others that bring out the worst. The mitzvahs are a Divine formula for creating ourselves by embracing the former and avoiding the latter.

This is the key to understanding Shabbat. It is a mitzvah comprising things we do and things we do not do, and our journey of self-creation on Shabbat emerges from their combination. We know what these things are from the *halacha* – Jewish law (the word *halacha* comes from the Hebrew word "to walk,"[3] perhaps alluding to the journey of self-transformation each mitzvah leads us through) as it emerges from the Talmud, and the commentaries and codifiers who followed. Shabbat cannot be separated from the *halacha*. When it is, Shabbat loses its Divine power and majesty, its meaning and uniqueness, and its ability to transform us.

At the most essential level, the *halacha* frames Shabbat as an immersive 25-hour experience beginning at sunset on Friday and ending as three medium-sized stars emerge in the night sky on Saturday, shaping that experience in two ways: what we do and what we don't do.

At the heart of what we don't do on Shabbat is what the Torah calls "work,"[4] which the *halacha* defines as 39 categories of creative actions,[5] encompassing the full spectrum of human innovation deployed to shape the environment to meet the needs of individuals and society. These categories relate to the production of the basic elements needed for human survival: food, clothing and shelter, as well as the resultant human imprint on the plant and animal world. They include the primary expressions of human creativity – writing, building and transporting, as well as the all-important category of igniting fire as a source of energy to provide light and heat, critical to the establishment of human civilization.

These categories are modeled, according to the Talmud, on the 39 forms of creative work employed to accomplish the first major architectural construction feat of Jewish history – building the ornate and intricate portable Sanctuary in the desert after the Exodus.[6] Each of the 39 has sub-categories,[7] and together they make up the laws of Shabbat, delineating what we refrain from doing on the day.[8]

Shabbat is, amongst other things, a day we refrain from household chores such as cooking, laundry, repairs, gardening[9] or shopping;[10] a day on which we do not go to work,[11] engage in commerce or handle money;[12] a day on which we do not build, write and transport objects; a day on which we do not ignite fire, switch on lights,[13] use electronic devices[14] or drive a car.[15]

The other dimension of Shabbat that shapes us is the actions we do – the positive experiences we curate under the direction of the *halacha*. We welcome in Shabbat by lighting candles before sunset, and we celebrate its sanctity with the words of Kiddush on a cup of wine on Friday night,[16] and with Havdalah when Shabbat goes out.[17] We eat three special festive meals – on Friday night, Shabbat day and then in the late afternoon[18] – sanctifying the meals with song, words of inspiration,[19] and delicious food.[20] We wear our best clothes,[21] indulge in the pleasures of rest,[22] and spend quality time together.[23] We recite special prayers,[24] read a special portion from the Torah,[25] and set aside time for Torah learning.[26] We talk[27] and walk[28] in ways that reflect the holiness and joy of the day.

The combination of what we do and what we don't do, of refraining and engaging, constitutes the perfect formula – designed by the One Who created us and knows us best – for creating ourselves by building character and shaping perspectives.

In this process of self-creation, we don't work alone – the spiritual energy of the day empowers us. On Shabbat, God infuses the world with intensified holiness and spiritual energy.[29] He also imbues us with what the Talmud[30] describes as an "extra soul" – an extra dimension of spirituality accessible to us only during Shabbat.[31] Objectively, Shabbat is different from any other day of the week. Its holiness was created at the beginning of time and stands independently of anything we do. But if we connect with it, we have the power to transform ourselves.

In the chapters that follow, we embark on a journey of discovering how we can create ourselves with Shabbat as our partner. The map of our journey is, as per the Ramban's philosophy,[32] divided into these two fundamental components of the human condition – character and perspectives.

The following two parts of this book explore how what we do and don't do on Shabbat refines our character so that we can become the best version of ourselves, and animates our perspectives on our lives and on our world. The next part looks at how self-creation itself leads to happiness, and how Shabbat grants us a Divine recipe for creating true and lasting happiness. And in the final part of the book, we reflect on the impact of Shabbat – its power to transform our lives and even to change the world.

Let the journey begin.

¹ This is an application of the Ramban's philosophy of mitzvahs discussed in the previous chapter. The Ramban's influence on Jewish thinking was immense – and enduring. Two generations later, one of the great sages of the era wrote a book applying the Ramban's approach systematically to each of the 613 mitzvahs. He published the work anonymously under the title "Sefer HaChinuch" (literally, the "Book of Education"), intending it as a book of instruction for his son. Even though the exact identity of the author is disputed, it is agreed that he was either a student of the Ramban or of the Rashba, himself a student of the Ramban. A recurring theme in this monumental classic is the importance of action as the platform for self-creation. See Sefer HaChinuch, mitzvot 16, 40, 264, 324.

² Talmud, Makkot 23b; see also Mechilta D'Rabbi Yishmael 23:13; Midrash Lekach Tov, Exodus 23:13.

³ See Sefer HeAruch, Halacha; Sefer HaTishbi, Halacha.

⁴ See Chapter 5 below.

⁵ Mishna, Shabbat 7:2; Talmud, Shabbat 31b, 73a, 97b; Midrash, Mechilta D'Rabbi Yishmael 35:1; Rambam, Mishne Torah, Hilchot Shabbat 7:1. The 39 categories are: Sowing, plowing, harvesting, gathering [sheaves of produce], threshing, winnowing, sorting, grinding, sifting, kneading, baking, shearing, laundering, combing, dyeing, spinning, warping a loom, threading heddles, weaving, unraveling, tying, untying, sewing, tearing, trapping, slaughtering, skinning, tanning, marking lines, smoothing, cutting to size, writing, erasing, building, demolishing, extinguishing fire, igniting fire, striking the final hammer blow, and carrying from one domain to another.

⁶ Jerusalem Talmud, Shabbat 7:2; Talmud, Shabbat 31b; see also Midrash, Lekach Tov, Numbers 7:88; Midrash, Yalkut Shimoni on Torah 146, 408; Rambam, Mishne Torah, Hilchot Shabbat 12:12; Tur, O.C. 358:1; Mishna Berura 316:38.

⁷ See Talmud, Bava Kama 2a; Talmud, Shabbat 2b; Talmud, Shevuot 5a.

⁸ The halacha is also made up of many laws promulgated by the Sanhedrin, which was given the Divine mandate to legislate in order to protect the mitzvah and its spirit. See Deuteronomy 17:11; Avot 1:1; Rambam, Sefer HaMitzvot, Positive Mitzvah 174, Negative Mitzvah 312; Rambam, Mishne Torah, Hilchot Mamrim, Chapter 1; Sefer HaChinuch, mitzvah 496.

⁹ There are many aspects of gardening included in the 39 categories of work. For example, sowing, includes any action that facilitates the

growth of plants (See Mishna Berura 336:51), such as watering (Talmud, Eruvin 104a; Rambam, Mishne Torah, Hilchot Shabbat 21:5; Shulchan Aruch, O.C. 336:3, 338:6), or pruning (Talmud, Shabbat 73b; Rambam, Mishne Torah, Hilchot Shabbat 7:3, 8:1-2).

[10] The Talmud, Beitza 36b-37a rules that transfer of ownership is forbidden on Shabbat. Such transactions contravene the prophetic instruction to dedicate the day to spiritual pursuits (Isaiah 58:13). Alternatively, transactions are Rabbinically forbidden as they often lead to writing down a record of the sale (Rashi).

[11] One's professional occupation generally entails performing one or more forbidden acts of work on Shabbat. There is also a general Rabbinic prohibition on receiving payment for work done on Shabbat (Talmud, Nedarim 37a; Talmud, Bava Metzia 58a; Rashi, Talmud, Ketubot 64a; Rambam, Mishne Torah, Hilchot Shabbat 6:25; Shulchan Aruch, O.C. 306:4). For exceptions to this see Shulchan Aruch O.C. 306:4-5. Additionally, Ramban (Leviticus 23:24, based on Talmud, Shabbat 24b-25a) teaches that engaging in commerce contravenes the Torah's instruction to reserve Shabbat as a day of rest.

[12] This forms part of a category of the Rabbinic decree to refrain from moving items meant only for weekday use (Talmud, Shabbat 123b), known as *muktzeh*, literally "put aside" [for weekday use], in order to maintain mindfulness of Shabbat (Rambam, Mishne Torah, Hilchot Shabbat 25:12). Money is an example of *muktzeh* (Rambam, Mishne Torah, Hilchot Shabbat 25:6; Mishna Berura 308:1, 308:13).

[13] An incandescent bulb houses a metal filament, which is ignited to glowing heat when the light switch is activated; thus, turning it on constitutes igniting a fire (Chazon Ish 50:9; Minchat Shlomo 1:12). Bulbs that do not produce heat are prohibited for reasons mentioned in the next note.

[14] The use of electricity potentially contravenes a number of the 39 categories of forbidden work; see Chazon Ish 50:9 for a comprehensive analysis of the issue. It may also contravene the Rabbinic laws of *molid*, creating something new (Beit Yitzchak Y.D. 2:1); or *tikkun maneh*, making a utensil usable (Chazon Ish 50:9). Furthermore, by using electricity, one contravenes the prohibition of *zilzul Shabbat*, disrespecting Shabbat (Igrot Moshe O.C. 4:60). In addition, it contravenes the obligation to adhere to *minhag Yisrael*, widespread Jewish practice (Minchat Shlomo 1:9).

[15] Driving a car involves the use of a spark plug and the burning of fuel which transgresses the prohibition of kindling a fire on Shabbat (Exodus 35:3).

[16] Talmud, Berachot 51b; Talmud, Pesachim 105b-106a; Talmud, Sukka 56a; Rambam, Mishne Torah, Hilchot Shabbat 29:6-7; Shulchan Aruch, O.C. 271:3-4, 10

[17] Talmud Berachot 27b, 33a, 52a; Talmud, Shabbat 150b-151a; Talmud, Pesachim 103b-104a, 106a; Rambam, Mishne Torah, Hilchot Shabbat 29:3, 29:24-29; Shulchan Aruch, O.C. 294-299

[18] Talmud, Shabbat 117b, based on Exodus 16:25; Rambam, Mishne Torah, Hilchot Shabbat 30:9; Shulchan Aruch, O.C. 291:1

[19] "The Seventh Day was Shabbat on which the Jewish People would eat and drink and start sharing words of Torah and singing praise to God." Talmud, Megilla 12b, based on Esther 1:10. For more on the custom to sing zemirot on Shabbat, see Machzor Vitry, Order of Shabbat 158; Sefer Chassidim 271; Taamei HaMinhagim 371.

[20] Talmud, Shabbat 118b, based on Isaiah 58:13; Rambam, Mishne Torah, Hilchot Shabbat 30:7; Shulchan Aruch, O.C. 242:1, 250:2.

[21] Talmud, Shabbat 113a; Rambam, Mishne Torah, Hilchot Shabbat 30:3; Shulchan Aruch, O.C. 262:2

[22] Tur, O.C. 290; Mishna Berura 4:36, 290:3

[23] Talmud, Megilla 12b, based on Esther 1:10. See also Shem MiShmuel, 5674 Vayakhel 6:16, based on Exodus 35:1 and Zohar 2:135a-b.

[24] Talmud, Berachot 28a, 30a; Talmud, Shabbat 119b; Talmud, Pesachim 117b; Rambam, Mishne Torah, Hilchot Tefilla 2:5, Seder HaTefilla 2:37; Tur, O.C. 292; Shulchan Aruch, O.C. 267, 286, 292, 487:1

[25] Jerusalem Talmud, Megilla 4:1; Talmud, Megilla 21a, 29b; Talmud, Bava Kama 82a; Rambam, Mishne Torah, Hilchot Tefilla 12:2, 12:6, 13:1; Shulchan Aruch, O.C. 135:1, 282

[26] See Chapter 7 below, note 13.

[27] Talmud, Shabbat 113b, 150a, based on Isaiah 58:13; Talmud, Avoda Zara 7a; Rambam, Mishne Torah, Hilchot Shabbat 24:1, 24:4; Shulchan Aruch, O.C. 307

[28] Talmud, Shabbat 113b, based on Isaiah 58:13; Talmud, Eruvin 38b; Rambam, Mishne Torah, Hilchot Shabbat 24:2-3; Shulchan Aruch, O.C. 301

Chapter Notes

[29] Eitz Chaim 40:15

[30] Talmud, Beitza 16a; Talmud, Taanit 27b; Tractate Sofrim 17:5

[31] On a basic level, the *neshama yeteira*, extra soul, means that on Shabbat a person has a greater capacity for relaxation, joy, and celebrating Shabbat with extra food and drink (Rashi, Talmud, Beitza 16a and Talmud, Taanit 27b). Sforno (Exodus 20:11, 31:17) says that this extra soul allows for greater service of God. The Rashba (Responsa 7:349) explains that every week the soul is recreated, starting on Sunday and reaching the zenith of its potential on Shabbat. The Kabbalistic sages explain that the soul consists of five components, not all of which are ordinarily accessible to the individual. The receiving of the *neshama yeteira* means that one is able to access the highest level of the soul, called the *Yechida* (Megaleh Amukot 175:1; Shelah, Toldot Adam, Beit Yisrael 17-18).

[32] As explained in Chapter 2 above.

CHARACTER

4 | Character

This part of the book is about how Shabbat builds our character – shaping us one character trait at a time. Character traits form our identity and shape our thinking, feelings and actions. What we do, how we engage with others, how we react to situations and the world around us is an expression of our character traits. If we are generous, we will give to others. If we are grateful, we will appreciate the people around us and express that appreciation. If we are humble, we will make space for God and other people in our lives.[1] If we are optimistic, everything we do will be permeated with energy and motivation.

Interestingly, the Hebrew word our sages use to describe character traits is *middot*,[2] which literally translates as measurements. Character traits are our measure. They are our *dimensions* as people. Just as our measurements – height, width, weight – describe us physically, our character traits describe us in moral and spiritual terms. In the physical world, what we can achieve with our bodies is in proportion to our physical dimensions and measurements; similarly, in the non-physical world, what we can achieve is in proportion to our *middot* – our spiritual measurements, our character traits.

The next 11 chapters of this book are dedicated to 11 character traits that keeping Shabbat cultivates (there are, surely, others), each drawn from the writings of our great rabbis over the ages. What emerges are 11 ways to refine our spiritual, moral and emotional state of being – our measurements of character.

Chapter Notes

[1] Talmud, Sota 5a; Talmud, Arachin 15b

[2] For examples see: Talmud, Chagiga 9b; Midrash, Tanchuma Buber, Appendix to Chukat 1:1; Midrash, Devarim Rabba 3:4; Midrash, Tanna D'Vei Eliyahu Zutta, additions to Seder Eliyahu Zutta, Mavo 33; Midrash Tehillim 1:8.

5 | Humble

In an ethical will to his son, the Ramban[1] writes:[2]

"What should a person be arrogant about? If he has wealth, it is God Who makes one prosperous... And if he has honor – does that not belong to God? If he takes pride in wisdom – let him understand that God can take away wisdom... Thus, all people stand as equals before their Creator."

Humility is the recognition that whatever we have comes from God alone,[3] and that we are not superior to any other person, because our achievements are gifts from our Creator. Success can lead to arrogance, as the verse says: "...lest you eat and become satisfied, and you build good houses and settle ... and your heart will become haughty and you will forget the Lord your God."[4]

The inclination toward arrogance is always present because human beings have God-given creative powers to harness and shape the world; the mandate to "fill the earth and conquer it, and rule over the fish of the sea, the birds of the sky, and every living thing that moves on the earth."[5] Utilizing these Divine powers, humanity has created awesome civilizations and breathtaking advances in every field of endeavor. And yet, these gifts can lead to arrogance,[6] or to an abuse of power, which can unleash destruction on the world. The human capacity to shape the world in accordance with our needs, wants, and ideas must be tempered by humility.

Keeping Shabbat leads us on the path to humility. On Shabbat, we suspend all our creative work – all acts of dominating the world, of imposing our will on our environment – and hand these powers back to God. Ceasing work on Shabbat is a statement of profound humility – an acknowledgement that God is the ultimate Creative Power in the universe, and that our own abilities to create and shape the world are God-given.[7]

We know that the Torah defines the work prohibited on Shabbat as *melacha*.[8] The common word for work, *avoda*, is related to the word *eved*, servant, and usually refers to hard labor. By contrast, *melacha* is related to the Hebrew word *mal'ach*, which is an angel or emissary (an angel is essentially a messenger of God).[9] Just as God sends an angel on a mission to fulfill His will in the world, when we do *melacha*, we impose our will on the world through a creative act.

When we keep Shabbat, we remember that God created the world in six days and rested on the seventh, and acknowledge His power and mastery over the world. The word Shabbat is related to the root of the Hebrew words "to judge" and "to place" – through ceasing our work, we place the world in the right order, justly attributing ultimate authority to God and understanding that we answer to Him. We submit our lives to God, and acknowledge that our powers and abilities, our creativity and innovation, are God-given, and that we should use them to fulfill His will.

But among the 39 categories of work, there is one that seems to resist our definition of *melacha* as creatively imposing our will on the world. It is the *melacha* of transferring an object from a private area to a public area[10] and vice versa (for example, taking an object from a house into the street, or the street into the house), and carrying an object in a public area.[11] These forms of carrying symbolize social interactions; the relationships between people, and between the individual and society. Not carrying is thus a call to also humbly submit our social interactions to Divine ethics. On Shabbat, we remember and reaffirm that God is the ultimate authority in nature *and* in human affairs.[12]

These two dimensions of Shabbat are reflected in the two historical reference points the Torah connects to Shabbat: God creating the world, and God freeing us from Egypt. Creation reminds us that He is the Source of all things, including our own creativity and achievements. The Exodus reminds us that God oversees our society, and that, therefore, our social interactions should also be under His guidance. Both teach us to be humble.

Humility is about recognizing the intrinsic value, appreciating the preciousness and the essential equality and dignity of every person created in the image of God. It is about recognizing that whatever gifts we may have come directly from God, and do not make us better than another person, but only impose on us greater responsibility to do good in the world.

In the letter to his son, the Ramban describes humility as "the finest of all character traits." And Shabbat enables us to cultivate it.

Chapter Notes

[1] Biographical information on the Ramban can be found in chapter 2 above.

[2] Iggeret HaRamban

[3] Pirkei Avot 3:8, based on I Chronicles 29:14

[4] Deuteronomy 8:12,14; see also Deuteronomy 8:17, 32:15; Talmud, Berachot 32a; Midrash, Sifrei, Devarim 318:1; Midrash, Lekach Tov, Deuteronomy 32:15.

[5] Genesis 1:28

[6] Deuteronomy 8:17

[7] The ideas of the next few paragraphs are drawn from Rabbi S.R. Hirsch. See his commentary on Genesis 2:1-3, Exodus 20:8-11, Deuteronomy 5:12-15, and in Horeb on the mitzvah of Shabbat.

[8] For example Exodus 20:9-10.

[9] Midrash, Bereishit Rabba 50:2

[10] Talmud, Shabbat 2a, 73a; Rambam, Mishne Torah, Hilchot Shabbat 12:9; Shulchan Aruch, O.C. 347:1

[11] Talmud, Eruvin 48a, 51a; Rambam, Mishne Torah, Hilchot Shabbat 12:15; Shulchan Aruch, O.C. 349

[12] Rabbi S.R. Hirsch, Exodus 35:1-2

6 | Still

When we are in a state of pressure, our decisions and actions can become instinctive, emotional and reflexive, without any real deliberation or sense of perspective. We may act rashly, stumbling, causing harm to others – and to ourselves. On top of this, anxiety and stress damage the body and cause us emotional pain.[1]

When we are calm and measured in thought and action – when we are still – we are able to decide wisely, act prudently, and live contentedly. Pirkei Avot teaches us to "be deliberate in judgment."[2] At a basic level, it refers to a judge who must carefully and dispassionately weigh the facts of a case, without rushing to conclusions, so that justice can be done.[3] But being "deliberate in judgment" is also a general principle for living wisely, and applies to our personal decisions,[4] big and small.

We make judgments about people and situations all the time, and these decisions can have serious consequences for ourselves and those around us. To "be deliberate" is to think something through patiently and deeply.[5] This tranquil state of mind allows for clarity of thought and rational analysis, which are crucial to good decision-making.[6]

To live wisely, we need to nurture inner calm. We need to be serene. This approach is useful in every aspect of life. The laws of Shabbat are designed by God to create an atmosphere conducive

31

to a state of being called *menucha* – a feeling of complete calm and serenity.[7] The opposite of *menucha* is *behala* – literally, panic, a state of frenzy and anxiety. Shabbat shields us from the forces that foment panic, confusion and instability, and creates time and space for us to regain our emotional and spiritual balance – to be still.

The greatest mistake of Jewish history was made in a state of frenzy and panic. 40 days after God spoke to the people at Sinai, they made a golden calf to worship in an act of rebellion that seems incomprehensible. It happened because they panicked when they thought that Moses, who had led them out of Egypt, would not be returning to them following his prolonged encounter with God on the mountain. In a state of intense anxiety and vulnerability, fearing for their survival in the desert, uncertain about their future, they lost their collective mind and fell into idolatry.[8]

The entire framework of restrictions and experiences of the Shabbat day is a formula for serenity. The 39 categories of work we don't do – and don't even speak about – bring relief. The carefully crafted moments of prayer and Torah learning bring us tranquility. The festive meals, candle-lighting, Kiddush, blessing children[9] – all of them combine to create the perfect formula for calm and stillness.

Shabbat also provides the strongest buffer against panic and anxiety – faith and trust in God.[10] When we feel held and looked after by God, we access the state of stillness. Trusting God means that we have complete peace of mind that the world and its events are not random and threatening – but are part of a loving plan orchestrated by God for the ultimate good, even when we cannot see how.[11]

Ultimately, this state of *menucha*, of supreme restfulness and tranquility, is the gateway to all the things that are most precious to us. The text of our Shabbat prayers[12] states that the *menucha* we access on Shabbat helps us live with "love and generosity", "truth and faith", and "peace, tranquility, stillness and trust." If we are flustered and under pressure, feeling anxious and frenzied, we do not have the emotional capacity for love, nor the openness for generosity. We lack the presence of mind for truth and faith, and the sense of stability to access stillness and trust.

Menucha is achieving a state of stillness, which is the gateway to physical, psychological, and spiritual well-being. And Shabbat is the gateway to *menucha* – to becoming still.

Chapter Notes

1   Rabbeinu Yona, Proverbs 14:30, 15:3, 17:22, 18:14

2   Pirkei Avot 1:1

3   Rabbeinu Yona, Avot 1:1

4   Tiferet Yisrael, Avot 1:1

5   Avot D'Rabbi Natan 1:4; Pirkei Avot 1:1 with Rashi, Rambam, Rabbeinu Yona

6   The idea of making decisions in a calm and tranquil state is expounded upon by Rabbi Chaim Shmuelevitz, Sichot Mussar, 43. See also Sichot Mussar, 55.

7   The ideas discussed in this chapter, that Shabbat provides a formula for *menucha* and how vital it is to well-being, are drawn from Rabbi Yerucham Levovitz, Daat Torah, Bereishit, p. 35-36, on Genesis 5:29.

8   Exodus 32:1-8, 23

9   Ma'avar Yabbok, Siftei Renanot 43; Sefer HaChaim, Parnasa V'Kalkala 6; Siddur of Rabbi Yichiah Salach; Siddur of Rabbi Yaakov Emden, Siddur Beit Yaakov, Shabbat Night 7; Siddur HaGra, Imrei Shefer, Shabbat Night

10   See Chapter 8 below.

11   Chazon Ish, Emunah U'Vitachon 2:1

12   Shabbat Mincha Amidah as explained by Rabbi Yerucham Levovitz, ibid.

7 | Wise

Being wise goes beyond being clever. It is about self-knowledge and self-awareness. It is about being perceptive of people and situations. To be wise is to understand the world and our place in it, integrating what we know into the way we live, bringing out the best in ourselves and others. Shabbat is a day set aside for us to become wiser.

Shabbat gives us the time to think and learn. And more than that – the day itself enriches our mind. When "God blessed the seventh day,"[1] He infused Shabbat with a unique spiritual energy through which we expand our knowledge, insight, and understanding – and attain wisdom.[2] We do that by learning Torah, enabling us to see the world through God's eyes.[3] In a world that can be murky and confusing, Torah learning grants us Divine wisdom, clarity, and direction,[4] inspiring us to lead a better life. For six days of the week, we pursue our material needs; working for the material means to sustain life in a material world. But on Shabbat, we dedicate ourselves to thinking and learning Torah, to becoming wiser.

Having at least one day a week to dedicate to the pursuit of wisdom is essential. When the Jewish People wandered the desert for 40 years, living by the daily miracles of God – Who provided them with water, food, and shelter[5] – they had ample time to learn Torah and imbibe its Divine wisdom.[6] Upon entering the Land of Israel, however, they realized everything was going to be different. "The land of milk and honey"[7] would need to be worked to produce its rich bounty – which meant time for spiritual pursuits would be limited. How could they keep their deep connection to Torah wisdom? When would they find time to learn?

The Midrash[8] vividly illustrates this dilemma through a 'conversation' in which the Torah complains to God:

"'Master of the Universe, when the Jewish People enter the Land of Israel, some will go to their vineyards and others to their fields – and what will become of me [how will they learn and know me]?'

God answered the Torah: 'I have a partner for you, and Shabbat is its name – because on Shabbat they will put their work on hold and be able to engage with you.'"

This Midrash refers to a dramatic transition that generation had to make. But Shabbat is God's answer to this challenge. He set it aside as a day to learn Torah and become wiser.[9]

The laws of Shabbat clear a full 25 hours from all the hassles and responsibilities of daily life, giving us not just the time, but the headspace to learn, to think, to pursue wisdom and knowledge. But we have to take the initiative and ensure we spend this time wisely. This is why the Torah tells us to "protect" the Shabbat.[10]

We can access great wisdom on Shabbat – but only through embracing the framework of laws that guard its sanctity, tranquility, and contemplative atmosphere. It is significant that the Torah calls on the Jewish People to "protect" Shabbat just as they are about to leave their desert existence and enter the Land of Israel. Their new working lifestyle would demand that they actively preserve Shabbat time for the pursuit of wisdom.[11] When we keep the laws of Shabbat, we build a fortress around the sacred time within.

It is true that we have a mitzvah to learn Torah every day[12] – but Shabbat is an ideal time. The Shulchan Aruch says that communities should, in fact, allocate time on Shabbat, not only for communal prayer, but also for communal learning, with public lectures on Torah ideas and laws.[13] Furthermore, if we pursue Divine wisdom on Shabbat, when we have the opportunity, we demonstrate our thirst for knowledge and wisdom, growth and inspiration.[14]

The way that Shabbat creates the time and space for us to think and learn is reflected in the very meaning of the word "Shabbat."[15] Shabbat means "to cease"[16] – to refrain from the 39 categories of work on Shabbat. But Shabbat also means "to reconsider" (the root word *shuv* literally means "to retract"/"reverse"/"return").[17] This refers to the process of learning – as we discover new knowledge and insights, we reverse our preconceptions and revise our understanding, seeing things from a new perspective. We contemplate what we know, pondering well-established ideas and considering new ones.

The dual meaning of the Hebrew word "Shabbat" – to cease, and to reconsider – is reflected in the dual dimensions of the day. By ceasing all work, as defined by the laws of Shabbat, we are free to reconsider our thinking, contemplating the truths of the world, gaining wisdom through learning Torah. This duality is also reflected in how the Torah sometimes refers to Shabbat in the plural ("My Sabbaths you shall keep.")[18]

The 'ceasing' and the 'reconsidering' we do on Shabbat are inseparable. Together they offer the opportunity for self-transformation by becoming wiser.

Chapter Notes

1 Genesis 2:3

2 Ibn Ezra, Exodus 20:8

3 Avot D'Rabbi Natan 4:1; Midrash, Bereishit Rabba 1:1; Zohar 2:161a

4 Talmud, Sota 21a, based on Proverbs 6:23, compares our world to a dark forest and the individual mitzvahs to lamps that shed limited light, while Torah learning is compared to the full light of day.

5 Exodus 16:35; Deuteronomy 8:3-4, 29:4-5; Leviticus 23:43 with Talmud, Sukka 11b; Nehemiah 9:15, 9:20

6 Midrash, Mechilta D'Rabbi Yishmael 13:17, 16:4; Midrash, Tanchuma, Beshalach 20:2

7 This description of the Land of Israel appears many times in the Torah, the first being Exodus 3:8.

8 The Chofetz Chaim (Mishna Berura 290:5) cites the Midrash in the name of the Tur, O.C. 290. This Midrash was originally part of the Midrash Abkir, the remnants of which can be found in the Midrash, Yalkut Shimoni on Torah 16:24 (see Biur HaGra, Shulchan Aruch, O.C. 290:2).

9 Jerusalem Talmud, Shabbat 15:3; Talmud, Pesachim 68b; Zohar 3:173a; Shulchan Aruch, O.C. 290:2; Mishna Berura 290:3, 4, 6, 7

10 Deuteronomy 5:12

11 The idea of "protecting" Shabbat as a day of learning is presented by Rabbi Meir Simcha of Dvinsk in his work Meshech Chochmah, Deuteronomy 5:12. He cites this as textual support for the important mandate to the sages to add Rabbinic laws to preserve the spirit of Shabbat.

12 Joshua 1:8; Mishna, Peah 1:1; Talmud, Berachot 35b; Rambam, Mishne Torah, Hilchot Talmud Torah 1:8; Shulchan Aruch, O.C. 155:1

13 Shulchan Aruch, O.C. 290:2, based on Jerusalem Talmud, Shabbat 15:3, as cited in Beit Yosef, O.C. 288:1

14 This observation of the Chofetz Chaim is presented both in Mishna Berura 290:7 and in Sifrei Chofetz Chaim, Shem Olam, Shaar Shemirat Shabbat ch. 5.

15 The ideas in the next few paragraphs are drawn from Rabbi Yaakov Tzvi Mecklenburg, HaKetav VeHaKabala, Exodus 20:10, 31:13.

16 For example, see Genesis 2:2; Leviticus 16:31.

[17] For example, see Deuteronomy 30:3; Numbers 13:26; Psalms 74:11; see also HaKetav VeHaKabbala, Exodus 20:10.

[18] Leviticus 19:30

8 | Trusting

Consider the following parable crafted by the Dubno Maggid, the great 18th century rabbi famous for enlivening deep philosophical ideas through colorful yet profound imagery:[1] A poor man is traveling along the road, carrying a heavy bag. Along comes a wealthy nobleman in a carriage drawn by horses, and offers a lift to the traveler, who accepts and climbs into the carriage. A short while later, the owner of the carriage notices that his new passenger is sitting with his heavy bag still on his shoulders. He says to him: "Why are you still carrying your bag? Why don't you put it down?"

The traveler answers: "I feel bad enough that you stopped to give me a lift and that your horses have the extra burden of my weight. The least I can do is carry my own bag."

The nobleman exclaims: "Don't be silly; the horses are carrying you and your bundles anyway."

On Shabbat, we remind ourselves that God carries us. We don't carry our burdens on our own. And on Shabbat, we can put them down.

Faith in God, a foundational mitzvah,[2] is brought into focus on Shabbat. We acknowledge God as the Creator of our world, Who took us out of Egypt and guides our destiny. Shabbat helps us transform faith from an intellectual understanding that God is in control, into trust, a feeling of security and confidence.

This trust does not mean we believe everything is going to turn out exactly the way we want; rather, it is the understanding that everything that happens in our lives is part of God's plan.[3] Whether we experience pain or pleasure, triumph or failure, abundance or scarcity, it is all part of God's plan for providing us with the experiences we need to fulfill our ultimate potential. As the Talmud puts it: "This, too, is for the good."[4] In being able to respond to life's vicissitudes, there is great comfort in knowing that life is not random, that God is in control and carrying us.

The psalm dedicated to Shabbat calls on us "to tell of Your kindness in the morning, and Your faithfulness at nights."[5] God cares for us in the bright optimism of the morning – times of ease, and during the dark nights – times of fear and uncertainty.[6] On Shabbat, we feel that intensely. It is a day of trust in God.[7] It is a day to recognize that our lives, and our burdens, are in God's hands.

This applies particularly to the natural anxiety we have about having the financial means to meet our basic needs. Shabbat specifically tests our trust in God in this area, because it is a day on which we set aside our money-making endeavors.[8] Peace of mind on Shabbat is only possible with complete trust in God. We do our best to earn a living during the week, but recognize that, ultimately, whatever we earn is by the blessings of God, Who is the source of everything in our lives.[9] We are, in a sense, God's salaried workers, and on Shabbat He gives us the day off – guaranteeing that our finances will not be affected – and lifts the burden of our anxieties.

God taught us this lesson of trust soon after we left Egypt,[10] when He introduced us to Shabbat – before we had even reached Sinai and received the Torah. Soon after, we began receiving our daily sustenance in the wilderness in the form of manna.[11] This miraculous food fell from the skies every morning and was preserved by dew until the people could gather it for their families. It fell daily, in just the right quantity for that day. Those who tried to hoard extra manna for later found that it had rotted.[12]

The exception was Friday. The Jewish People were told that two portions of manna per household would fall on Friday so that they would have enough for Shabbat. They were told not to gather manna on Shabbat, a holy day. Instead, the manna collected on Friday remained perfectly fresh throughout Shabbat.[13] This is why we place two challahs on the table at each meal, reminding us of the double portion of manna that fell on Friday for Shabbat.[14] One of the reasons we cover the bread is to remember the dew of the wilderness that protected the manna.[15]

When the Torah says that God "blessed the Shabbat",[16] it refers to the blessing of manna from heaven.[17] Manna represents the trust the Jews in the wilderness had in God as they patiently waited for their sustenance from day to day. By instructing the people to gather a double portion on Friday and then nothing on Shabbat, God was testing their willingness to respect the laws of Shabbat and to trust that He would provide. The manna was essentially a test of faith.[18] Many generations later, the prophet Jeremiah called the people's attention to the jar of manna,[19] which had been preserved as a symbol to future generations – of what it means to have complete trust in God for one's sustenance.[20]

Each week, seeing the two challahs on our Shabbat tables, we remember how God provided for our people in the desert for 40 years,[21] and that our own sustenance today is just as miraculous – that it comes from heaven even if it doesn't fall out of the sky. We try to model our ancestors' serene faith – how, despite being in the most vulnerable circumstances, they felt at peace, confident that God would look after them.

CHARACTER

Shabbat trains us to be trusting people – to trust God, to feel secure and confident that our lives are in His hands. It's not just about our concerns for sustenance, but every aspect of our well-being, including health, family, success, and safety – we rely on God for it all.[22] Our aim is to carry this feeling of trust with us into the week, and to let it infuse every part of our lives, every blessing we enjoy. We may no longer be wandering in the wilderness, but our future is equally unknown and unknowable, and, fundamentally, we are just as vulnerable.

Each week, Shabbat instills in us trust in God to meet an uncertain future with confidence. This is reflected in a beautiful custom during the final moments of Shabbat when we sing the words of Psalms chapter 23,[23] which have provided comfort through the ages: "Even when I walk through the valley of the shadow of death, I shall fear no evil, for You are with me."[24]

And then on Saturday night, as we venture out from the security of Shabbat into the unknowns of the week, we are fortified with a renewed faith in God, instilled in us over the course of the day. Shabbat culminates with the confident declaration of the words of the prophet Isaiah we proclaim as we introduce Havdalah: "Behold, God is my salvation, I shall trust and not fear – for God is my might and my praise."[25]

1. Rabbi Yaakov Krantz, the Dubno Maggid, Ohel Yaakov, Parshat Yitro, on Exodus 20:8, s.v. *ume'ata*

2. Rambam, Sefer HaMitzvot, Positive Mitzvah 1, based on Exodus 20:2

3. Chazon Ish, Emunah U'Vitachon 2:1

4. Talmud, Taanit 21a; Talmud, Sanhedrin 108b-109a

5. Psalms 92:3

6. Rashi, Psalms 92:3

7. Zohar 2:92a, 3:94b, 3:288b; Ramban, Exodus 20:8; Radak, Psalms 92:3

8. Midrash, Mechilta D'Rabbi Yishmael 20:9, based on Exodus 20:9

9. Talmud, Berachot 33b; Talmud, Megilla 25a; Talmud, Nidda 16b; see also: Jerusalem Talmud, Taanit 3:11, based on Psalms 136:25; Jerusalem Talmud, Pesachim 5:7, based on Psalms 136:25; Talmud, Taanit 2a-b, based on Psalm 145:16; Talmud, Pesachim 118a, based on Psalms 136:25.

10. 10 days after leaving Egypt; Exodus 15:22.

11. This took place 20 days later; Exodus 16:1-4.

12. Exodus 16:22-30

13. See Exodus 16:22-24.

14. Talmud, Shabbat 117b

15. Tosafot on Talmud, Pesachim 100b

16. Genesis 2:3

17. Rashi, Genesis 2:3

18. Exodus 16:4

19. Midrash, Mechilta D'Rabbi Yishmael 16:33; Rashi, Jeremiah 2:31

20. Rashi, Exodus 16:32

21. Exodus 16:35; Deuteronomy 8:3-4, 29:4-5; Nehemiah 9:15, 9:20

22. Psalms 145:16

23. Bnei Yissaschar, Shabbatot, 8:17, in the name of the Arizal

24. Psalms 23:4

25. Isaiah 12:2

9 | Gentle

Conflict is destructive. It brings tension and distance to our precious relationships. Like a destructive fire, it consumes happiness, love and connection, the very foundations of a home.

The Torah tells us: "Do not burn fire in your homes on Shabbat."[1] Beyond a basic instruction about keeping Shabbat, the Zohar says this also alludes to the fires of anger and conflict.[2] Shabbat must be a time of love and peace and togetherness, not fragmentation and dispute and tension.[3]

The candles we light to usher in Shabbat were instituted by our sages to create a tranquil atmosphere at home.[4] What our sages term "peace of the home"[5] is sacrosanct, which is why if a person cannot afford both Chanukah candles and Shabbat candles, the latter take precedence, even though the Chanukah candles are lit to publicize the Divine miracles that occurred.[6] The peace between husband and wife is especially sacred – to the extent, says the Talmud, that God allows His sacred Name to be erased if that is necessary to preserve harmony between them.[7]

Shabbat candles preserve peace in a very practical way – by illuminating the space we live in so that we are spared the distress of stumbling about in darkness, and the conflict that ensues.[8] But perhaps the candles symbolize "peace of the home" in a deeper way: they create an atmosphere of tranquility, allowing us to savor the experience of being together on Shabbat, seeing each

47

other's faces, so that we can really connect. In this way, Shabbat candles symbolize the light of love and attention. The pressures of the week place demands on our time and divert our attention from the people closest to us. The light of the candles helps us re-establish that intimate connection.

Seeing each other – really *seeing* each other – nurtures empathy, and is the secret to overcoming anger and resentment. "Judge every person favorably," says Pirkei Avot.[9] In the original Hebrew there is a powerful nuance that allows for another reading of the words "every person" to mean "the *entire* person."[10] Judging someone favorably comes naturally when we see them in full context – when we keep in mind that their lives, like our own, are inevitably more complicated than they seem on the surface. We recognize that we cannot possibly know all of the circumstances behind someone's behavior, and that we should view their perceived faults in the broader context of the good they do. Shabbat gives us the time and space to truly see those around us – especially our loved ones – and relate to them with empathy and compassion, generosity and kindness, love and closeness.

On Shabbat, we nurture the stillness to notice and appreciate the people in our lives. When our hearts are peaceful, so are our homes. On Shabbat, we can achieve peace of mind, a sublime inner restfulness that creates the ideal state for love and connection. It is not just a superficial calm and tranquility, but a deep state of being that is unflustered and undistracted, gentle and kind, open to connection and love.

The polar opposite of this spirit of peace and stillness is anger, which the Talmud says is one of the most destructive forces in a person, robbing us of wisdom and good judgment.[11] Generally, we are advised in developing our character traits to avoid that which is extreme and aim for the "middle path."[12] There are, however, two exceptions – two areas where balance is not the ideal. One is arrogance; we should always strive to be extremely humble. And the other is anger; we should always seek to be extremely forbearing and self-possessed.[13]

As the Ramban advised his son in his ethical will: "Accustom yourself always to speak all of your words with gentleness to all people at all times, and through this you will be saved from anger, which is a terrible trait that causes people to sin."[14] He teaches us that whatever rage we are feeling on the inside, we should model the opposite on the outside – for, by speaking gently, we can actually calm our emotions. When we look at the Shabbat candles, we remind ourselves of this.

Peace and gentleness are the heart and soul of the Torah value system[15]– as the Book of Proverbs says: "Her ways are ways of pleasantness, and all of her paths are those of peace."[16] Shabbat brings the light of peace and gentleness, of love and connection, into our character, our homes, and our way of life.

Chapter Notes

1 Exodus 35:3

2 Tikkunei Zohar 85a

3 The ideas in this chapter are based on Rabbi Chaim Shmuelevitz, Sichot Mussar, 54.

4 Talmud, Shabbat 23b

5 Talmud, Shabbat 23b: '[Shabbat] candles take precedence on account of peace of the home.'

6 Rambam, Mishne Torah, Hilchot Megilla 4:14; Shulchan Aruch, O.C. 296:5, based on Talmud, Shabbat 23b

7 Numbers 5:11-23. This unprecedented erasure of God's name is discussed in: Jerusalem Talmud, Sota 1:4; Talmud, Shabbat 116a; Talmud, Sukka 53b; Talmud, Nedarim 66b; Talmud, Makkot 11a; Talmud, Chullin 141a. See also Talmud, Berachot 54a, based on Ruth 2:4.

8 Rashi, Talmud, Shabbat 25b; see also Rashi, Talmud, Shabbat 23b.

9 Pirkei Avot 1:6

10 Sfat Emet, Pirkei Avot 1:6. The Hebrew term *kol ha'adam* in the context of the Mishna means "every person" but can be translated as "the entire person."

11 Talmud, Pesachim 66b

12 Rambam, Mishne Torah, Hilchot Deot 1:4-7, 2:2-3; Shemona Perakim, Chapter 4

13 Rambam, Mishne Torah, Hilchot Deot 2:3

14 Iggeret HaRamban

15 See Talmud, Gittin 59b, which states that "the entire Torah is for the sake of peace."

16 Proverbs 3:17

10 | Generous

Shabbat can help us overcome the most destructive aspects of human nature. Pirkei Avot lists them as jealousy, the desire for physical pleasure, and the pursuit of honor, and tells us that they "drive a person from the world."[1] The common denominator here is self-centeredness – begrudging that which pertains to others (jealousy); the relentless pursuit of self-gratification (desire); and valuing others only inasmuch as they provide recognition and attention to us (the pursuit of honor).[2]

Generosity of spirit is the very opposite of selfishness. It is the willingness to give and share, to support and help. Being generous is the capacity to move beyond the self.

Self-centeredness is, paradoxically, self-destructive – it "drives a person from the world," meaning from both this world and the next.[3] The commentators explain that jealousy, desire and the pursuit of honor destroy a person's quality of life.[4] Jealousy wreaks both physiological and emotional damage – it devours a person from the inside.[5] Unbridled self-indulgence can lead to excesses that are damaging to a person's physical and emotional health.[6] The relentless pursuit of honor causes conflict between people, which disturbs peace of mind.

These three driving forces within the human being are also the root of much wrongdoing.[7] Jealousy deters people from dealing ethically, compassionately and sensitively with others. When people are consumed with self-gratification, they act in ways counter to the innate sanctity and dignity with which God has bestowed human beings. And the craven pursuit of honor and recognition drives people to violate their most basic values and principles, and to betray their conscience. Together, they drive a person not just from this world, but from the World to Come.

The Torah records how these negative forces caused cataclysmic destruction among the early generations of human history.[8] The first sin of history was caused by desire, when Adam and Eve ate the forbidden fruit from the Tree of Knowledge.[9] In the following generation, it was jealousy that spurred Cain to take the life of his brother, Abel, whose sacrifices were favored by God.[10] The destruction of the flood was brought about by a generation steeped in jealousy – which led to theft, unethical behavior and even violence, and also self-gratification – expressed in the rampant sexual immorality that characterized that generation.[11] The generation of the Tower of Babel suffered their downfall in pursuit of honor,[12] in their obsession with building an enormous edifice to bring them fame and glory.

These forces of self-centeredness can be difficult to overcome because they are ingrained in human nature. In fact, the reason that Pirkei Avot singles out these three specific forces is because God has planted them within us, and we are naturally prone to them.[13] At the same time, God has given us the means to overcome these forces and become more generous people. One of these means is Shabbat.

God has given us the incredible gift of Shabbat as the counter-balance to jealousy, desire and the pursuit of honor – symbolized by the three holy meals of Shabbat – and as a force for nurturing generosity within us.[14]

How does Shabbat counter these forces of negativity?

Firstly, Shabbat helps us control and channel our physical desires. We don't repress sensory pleasure; it's a natural part of who we are. We harness it in healthy and positive ways and connect it to sanctity and a higher purpose.[15] When physical desire controls us, we become overwhelmed by it, unable even to enjoy it; but when we can control physical desire, it brings us joy.

Shabbat also helps us overcome jealousy. It does this by ingraining in us trust in God, symbolized by the two challahs on the Shabbat table for each of the meals, which remind us of how He looked after our ancestors in the desert.[16] Trusting God entails a belief in a world of abundance, that everything is the way it should be by Divine plan, that what we have is what we need, and what others have is what *they* need. By making peace with our lives and what we have in this way, we can overcome the forces of jealousy.[17]

Shabbat also helps us contain our need for honor and recognition. Shabbat cultivates humility in us,[18] helps us recognize God's greatness, thereby enabling us to set aside our pursuit of honor. Being humble is recognizing that we are not superior to others; we are all equal, created in God's image,[19] and therefore honor and recognition are illusory, and any attempt to lord over others is sheer vanity.[20]

Shabbat is the Divine formula to help us overcome the three destructive forces of "jealousy, desire and honor," rooted in self-centeredness. Shabbat nurtures within us the counterforce to selfishness – a spirit of generosity and benevolence, of transcending the self.

Chapter Notes

[1] Pirkei Avot 4:28

[2] Tiferet Yisrael, Avot 4:28

[3] Ibid.

[4] Magen Avot, Avot 4:28; see also Pirkei Moshe, Avot 4:28.

[5] Proverbs 6:34, 14:30, 24:1-2, 27:4; Job 5:2; Song of Songs 8:6; Ecclesiastes 4:4

[6] Meiri, Pirkei Avot 2:7

[7] See Abarbanel, Avot 4:28.

[8] Rabbi S.R. Hirsch, Genesis 11:4

[9] Genesis 3:6

[10] Genesis 4:3-8

[11] Genesis 6:11-13; Talmud, Sanhedrin 57a; Midrash, Bereishit Rabba 28:8

[12] Genesis 11:4

[13] See Yaavetz, Avot 4:28.

[14] The Sochatchover Rebbe, Shem MiShmuel, 5671 Noach 1, quotes Tikkunei Zohar 140a, which says that Noah is symbolically linked to Shabbat and that Shabbat can protect us from these three negative forces, just as the Ark protected Noah. This chapter is premised on that basic idea, but takes the liberty of elaborating on it.

[15] See Chapter 35 below.

[16] See Chapter 8 above.

[17] See Ibn Ezra, Exodus 20:14, based on Talmud, Moed Katan 28a.

[18] See Chapter 5 above.

[19] Genesis 1:26-27, 9:6; Pirkei Avot 3:18

[20] See Iggeret HaRamban; see also Ecclesiastes 6:2.

11 | Optimistic

We all need hope. King David, one of the greatest leaders of Jewish history, experienced devastating hardship and suffering in his life, and expressed the deep human need for hope when he said: "Hope in God – let your heart be strong and courageous, and hope in God."[1]

These words, which he composed in his Book of Psalms, describe a virtuous cycle of hope and courage. Hope builds courage, and courage breeds hope, and together they nurture optimism – a profound confidence in the future.

King David earned the right to talk about optimism because during his life he faced daunting problems and unspeakable pain. He was pursued by King Saul,[2] endured wars[3] and famine[4] as a leader, suffered the deaths of several of his children[5] and faced an armed rebellion against his rule by his own son.[6] And after all that, he remained full of hope, explaining that his source of hope was faith in God – the confidence and comfort we take in knowing that we are in His loving embrace and that whatever happens is somehow, even if we cannot see it, part of His eternal plan.

Hope is vital to fulfilling our Divine mission.[7] When we feel weakened and discouraged, we lack the resolve to do good. Even Joshua, who succeeded Moses as the leader of the Jewish People, needed constant encouragement.[8] God told Joshua: "Be strong and courageous."[9] The double reference to strength and courage refers to the two stages of any endeavor – starting something and seeing it through to completion with sustained resolve.[10] Joshua was a great leader; he not only witnessed God's miracles first-hand, but was brave enough to take an opposing stand to the other spies' slanderous reports about the Land of Israel.[11] If someone as courageous as Joshua needed encouragement, then certainly we need it too.

Shabbat gives us courage and strength – it gives us hope – because it imbues us with faith. It reminds us that God created the universe[12] – that as its loving, benevolent Creator, He is its ultimate master – and also of God's ultimate declaration of optimism when He completed His work on the sixth day just before bringing in Shabbat: "And God saw everything He had created, and behold it was very good."[13]

Shabbat also reminds us of the deeply optimistic notion of a World to Come – where there will be ultimate reward for the righteous, and all the pain of this world will be righted.[14] We see this in a special psalm, dedicated as a "song for the day of Shabbat,"[15] which Moses composed while still in Egypt, to give the Jews the hope and encouragement they needed to face their ongoing slavery.[16] They were troubled by how Pharaoh could inflict suffering on them with impunity.[17] In response, through this psalm, Moses, with prophetic insight, confronts the pain and confusion of seeing injustice in the world, and expresses comfort that, ultimately, God ensures there will be justice – not primarily in this world, but in the next, the eternal world.[18] This moving psalm comforted the Jewish People on Shabbat when they had the time to reflect on these optimistic ideas of faith and trust.

Finally, Shabbat reminds us that human history will culminate in the triumph of the values of faith, compassion, and wisdom, and in a world of peace and prosperity in which God's presence is manifest throughout creation.[19]

In short, Shabbat provides us with a profoundly optimistic worldview. The week is full of uncertainty; we struggle along, dealing with various pressures and difficulties. But one thing is certain: when the sun sets on Friday afternoon, Shabbat comes in. No matter what else is going on in our lives, Shabbat always arrives. It is an authentically optimistic cycle to live in because it always culminates in the light, joy, and inspiration of Shabbat. No matter what happens during the week, the love and joy and faith and peace of Shabbat is no more than six days away.

We move through the week with our eyes on Shabbat: a day of courage and hope – a day of optimism.

Chapter Notes

[1] Psalms 27:14

[2] I Samuel 17-31

[3] See I Kings 5:17; I Chronicles 28:3.

[4] II Samuel 21:1

[5] II Samuel 12:18, 13:23-29, 18:14

[6] II Samuel 15-19

[7] The idea and example in this paragraph are drawn from Rabbi Simcha Zissel Ziv Broide, Kitvei HaSaba MiKelm, Yamim Noraim 4.

[8] See Deuteronomy 31:7

[9] Deuteronomy 31:23, Joshua 1:6, 1:9

[10] Malbim, Joshua 1:6

[11] Numbers 14:6-10

[12] Exodus 20:11

[13] Genesis 1:31

[14] See Chapter 25 below at length on these ideas.

[15] Psalm 92

[16] Talmud, Bava Batra 14b states that a number of chapters of Psalms were composed by Moses. Rashi there and in Psalms 90:1 states that the psalms composed by Moses are Psalms 90-101. Rabbi Yaakov Kamenetsky, Emet LeYaakov, Exodus 5:9, says that the scrolls the Jewish People would read on Shabbat, mentioned in the Midrash, Shemot Rabba 5:18, contained these psalms. See Chapter 13 below, note 8.

[17] Emet LeYaakov, Exodus 5:9

[18] Rashi, Psalms 92:1

[19] See Chapter 27 below.

12 | Growing

Fulfilling our potential requires constant growth and self-improvement. Shabbat nurtures within us this growth mindset. It reconnects us to the source of all human development – the Divine soul within.

The spiritual energy of Shabbat grants us an "extra soul."[1] At Havdalah, as the holiness of the day departs, we symbolically acknowledge the loss of this added Shabbat soulfulness by smelling invigorating spices to revive our spirit.[2] Smell is the most spiritual of our physical senses.[3] It is less essential to our physical well-being than hearing, sight, touch, and taste, and has a certain ethereal quality – fragrances are largely intangible and indiscernible.

Inhaling spices reminds us of the Divine soul within each of us and how Shabbat connects us to it. This is important because the soul is the source of all human greatness – the fount of our awesome potential, which it is our life's mission to actualize.

When our soul comes to this world, it is pure potential, untested by the challenges of living in a physical body in a physical world, with temptation and free choice. Our life's journey – the very purpose for which we are created – is to be constantly growing and developing ourselves, giving birth to our deep inner potential by becoming people of wisdom, faith, integrity, compassion, humility, and so much more. Our blueprint for doing so is the

Torah and its commandments – the Divine plan of action for developing our potential.[4]

That is why the human being was given the name "Adam," from the Hebrew for "earth."[5] At first glance, this appears coun-terintuitive, since we primarily identify with our sublime souls rather than our earthly bodies. But there is, in fact, an intrinsic connection between human beings and the earth: they are both pure potential. Whether a piece of land will produce fruit depends on what is done with it. Even the most fertile land will not produce fruit if it is left to lie fallow; it needs to be plowed, fertilized, and irrigated. So, too, the human being is pure potential, and to live a fruitful, productive life of growth and improvement requires continuous work and development.

We have been given free choice to turn that potential into personal growth; to accumulate mitzvahs and attain spiritual greatness. We can choose to squander it and simply let it lie dormant. Or we can spend a lifetime growing and actualizing our awesome Divine potential.

To be human is to be called to constant upward motion. The prophet Zechariah refers to human beings as "walkers," and to angels as "standers."[6] How do we understand this? Because angels are purely spiritual with no capacity for wrongdoing,[7] they are perfect yet static.[8] They are who they are, and they are unchanging. Human beings are imperfect, full of flaws – yet with the capacity to improve and become great. And it is this dynamism of the human being that is captured in the word "walkers." Our lives are a journey of growth.

Shabbat, the day we have an "extra soul," is the day of growing ourselves. We pray, learn, listen, and think. We give, share, and connect. We stop doing and start becoming. We nurture a growth mindset. We rededicate ourselves to actualizing our God-given potential. And we usher it out with spices – as a comfort for losing our extra soul, and as a reminder to continue walking the upward path toward our best selves.

Chapter Notes

[1] For sources and explanation on this concept see Chapter 3 above, note 31.

[2] Zohar 2:208b, 3:35b; Maharal, Netivot Olam, Netiv HaTorah 10:8, 10:20; Taamei HaMinhagim 409

[3] Talmud, Berachot 43b

[4] The ideas in these paragraphs are based on Rabbi Yehuda Loew ben Betzalel, Maharal, Tiferet Yisrael, Chapter 3.

[5] See Genesis 2:7.

[6] Zechariah 3:7

[7] Rambam, Guide for the Perplexed, Part 2:7; Ohr HaChaim, Genesis 1:1; Akeidat Yitzchak 8:3; Shelah, Toldot Adam; Maharal, Derech Chaim on Avot 3:19; Derech Hashem 2:1:3; Yaarot Devash, 1:2

[8] See Rabbi S.R. Hirsch, Collected Writings IV, p. 68; see also Nefesh HaChaim 1:10; Likutei Torah, Shelach.

13 | Rooted

As human beings, we seek roots – the sense of being connected to something enduring.[1] This struggle takes us back to the very origins of humankind, birthed in the pain of rootlessness. "You will be a nomad and a wanderer on earth"[2] was the Divine punishment Cain suffered after murdering his brother Abel. Such a state of being felt unbearable to him, and when he cried out, God gave Cain a "sign."[3] The Midrash[4] connects this to the moment, millennia later, when God introduces the mitzvah of Shabbat as a "*sign* between Me and the children of Israel."[5]

The Midrash explains that this means that God gave Cain the chance to repent, to return to a path of virtue, through the healing power of Shabbat. During the week, Cain would indeed be "a nomad and a wanderer," lost in the confusion of a material world. But once a week, God granted him the opportunity to root himself in Shabbat – to tether himself to eternal values and return to his essential goodness. The Midrash describes the poignant moment when Adam, Cain's father, encounters him after the traumatic murder, and how Cain tells his father of his repentance.[6] Adam is so overcome that he composes a psalm[7] in honor of Shabbat.[8]

Shabbat offers a chance for us to return to our spiritual roots – to repent and begin anew. The root of the Hebrew word for repentance means "to return." True repentance is about returning to our essential God-given goodness. With its meaningful spiritual moments and contemplative tranquility, its focus on faith and purpose, and the space it gives us to enrich our most precious relationships, Shabbat helps us return to our true selves. It roots us and nurtures us spiritually, which is the deeper meaning of menucha.[9]

Menucha, superficially translated as rest, is the deep sense of rootedness that comes with being connected to the enduring values of the Torah. God refers to the Jewish People as "the branch of My planting."[10] The Talmud says that "the branch of My planting" also refers to the World to Come.[11] When we connect with God by fulfilling His commandments, we plant ourselves in eternity. Shabbat is a day rooted in eternity, or, as the Talmud describes it, "a taste of the World to Come."[12]

The search for emotional and spiritual roots goes to the heart of the human condition. There are two ways of relating to God, and to our lives in general – as a nomad and as a settler.[13] Let's explore this analogy.

Initially, human beings were nomads, before transitioning to building settlements, villages and cities. The shift was profound. Nomads allow their livestock to graze wherever the grazing is good, and move on when the grass runs out or the water runs low. Settlers, however, remain rooted in the village, even if the crops are meager and the weather grim.

These two modes of existence come from completely different mindsets. Nomads lack commitment to the place they are in, essentially living a parasitic existence, taking what is beneficial, but moving on when the benefits cease. In addition, because nomads are always on the move, they form no feelings of attachment to a particular place.

Settlers, on the other hand, form strong emotional bonds with the places they live in, and this bond persists through good times and bad – this is what it means to have a home. The settler's sense of self is shaped by his attachment to the place he lives. For the nomad, a place is merely a convenient, temporary geographic location, useful only inasmuch as it satisfies the nomad's needs. For the settlers, their identity is connected to where they live. It is a mental, emotional – even spiritual – bond.

These two paradigms of human existence – the nomad and the settler – permeate our relationships and even our self-identity. How do we relate to our loved ones? The nomadic mindset can undermine all our most precious relationships. If we approach marriage or parenting with the mindset of a nomad, we become emotionally selfish, we lack real commitment to our loved ones, and as a result, we lack real love and attachment.

Yet, the life of the nomad is alluring. There is a part of us that seeks to take as much benefit from the world, from God, and from people, as we can, at the least cost. But this emotional or spiritual rootlessness is profoundly disturbing to the human psyche. We crave permanence, a real connection to something greater and more enduring than ourselves.

When it comes to our relationship with God, the same questions arise. Are we spiritual nomads who connect only when convenient, or does our commitment run deeper? Are we emotionally invested 'settlers', whose identity is bound up with our Divine values, or are we transient spiritual travelers? We may see the benefits of Torah wisdom and choose to partake of it, but then we do so as a spiritual nomad, without it shaping our identity and vision. A spiritual nomad cannot form a real bond with God, because a one-sided relationship is not a relationship at all. On the other hand, if we embrace our Jewish identity as central to who we are, as the place we plant our spiritual roots, then we truly connect with God.

One of God's Names is "The Place."[14] The Midrash explains this name: "The world is not the place of God, but God is the Place of the world."[15] God contains the universe; He is not contained by it. This also means that God is our "Place" in life – that our connection to God should not be one of expedience, but immersive, unconditional, committed, where we live. We need to nurture that sense of rootedness. With such a connection, our very identity becomes intertwined with our relationship with God.

Shabbat enables us to nurture the character trait of being rooted and committed. It roots us in our eternal Divine values, and is a totally immersive experience; a self-contained world that connects us to God. This sense of connectedness to all things sacred that we experience on the day gives meaning to our existence.

Shabbat reorients the directionless drift of our lives and roots us in eternity.

[1] The ideas of the next paragraphs about being rooted in Shabbat are drawn from Rabbi Sholom Noach Berezovsky, the Slonimer Rebbe, Netivot Shalom, Parshat Bereishit, p. 29.

[2] Genesis 4:12

[3] Genesis 4:15

[4] Midrash, Tanchuma, Bereishit 10

[5] Exodus 31:17

[6] Midrash, Bereishit Rabba 22:13

[7] Psalms 92

[8] Midrash, Bereshit Rabba 22:13; Midrash, Vayikra Rabba 10:5; Midrash, Pesikta D'Rav Kahana 24:11. See Midrash, Pirkei D'Rabbi Eliezer 19:3 which explains that after Adam composed the psalm it was subsequently forgotten and Moses prophetically rediscovered it. See Chapter 11 above, note 16.

[9] The idea that the *menucha* of Shabbat roots us spiritually is explained by Rabbi Yerucham Levovitz, Daat Torah, Bereishit, p. 35-36, on Genesis 5:29.

[10] Isaiah 60:21

[11] Talmud, Sanhedrin 90a

[12] Talmud, Berachot 57b

[13] This analogy and the ideas that follow are drawn from Rabbi Yosef Dov Soloveitchik, in his article "Sacred and Profane."

[14] HaMakom; the first time this name features in the Talmud is in Mishna, Berachot 5:1.

[15] Midrash, Bereishit Rabba 68:9; Midrash, Pesikta Rabbati 21:1; Midrash, Tehillim 90:6; Midrash, Lekach Tov, Genesis 28:11

14 | Idealistic

Why do we do what we do? Are we driven by self-interest or higher ideals?

God tested Abraham, commanding him to leave his birthplace for "the land I will show you,"[1] the Land of Israel. Emigration is an extremely trying experience. A person has to start afresh in entirely new surroundings, leaving behind all that is familiar and comfortable, potentially negatively impacting a person's family, social, and financial circumstances.[2]

To counteract these difficulties, God promises Abraham great blessings for making the move: "I will make you into a great nation, and I will bless you and make your name great, and you will be a blessing."[3] Essentially, God tells Abraham he would emerge more enriched than if he had not left in the first place.

This is captured in the words God says to Abraham: "Go for yourself."[4] The journey God sends Abraham on is for his own benefit.[5] By leaving his birthplace, as God commands, Abraham will make a historic contribution to human civilization and to the establishment of the Jewish People, and will attain great wealth and renown. If he stays where he is, he will remain childless and be forgotten from history.

That was Abraham's test. God said to him, go to the Land of Israel.[6] There were extraordinary benefits for him in doing so – but could he do it for higher motives, for the sake of his ideals? Pirkei Avot teaches us that Abraham passed this test among nine other tests of his character and faith – he went, idealistically, out of loyalty and devotion to God.[7]

We see from this that situations of blessing and abundance can be their own test.[8] Self-sacrifice in order to do the right thing is one kind of test, but when there's actually benefit in choosing right, the challenge shifts. Are we doing it for the sake of God – because it's the right thing to do and the purpose for which we were created? Or are we doing it for personal benefit?

Shabbat teaches us to be idealistic; to set aside self-serving motivations and do the right thing for its own sake. The Torah instructs us: "Remember the Shabbat day to make it holy."[9] In reference to this verse, the Talmud explains that we need to *remember* Shabbat because it can be forgotten.[10]

There's a deeper meaning here. Shabbat is a remarkable day. There is an abundance of personal benefits of keeping Shabbat. But *why* do we keep it? Is it a lifestyle choice? Or do we keep Shabbat because God said we should, to remember that He created the world, to declare our faith in Him? "Remember Shabbat" – don't forget to sanctify it, to preserve the holiness of Shabbat by making it a day of faith and sacred pursuits, and keeping it because it is a mitzvah.

Of course, it's not a binary choice. Human beings are complex, we're motivated by many things all at once. Every decision we make exists on the spectrum from idealism to self-interest. It is difficult to be purely idealistic in all that we do – but we need to be moving in that direction. In fact, the Talmud itself says that a person should do the mitzvahs even for self-serving reasons, as this will, ultimately, lead to doing them for the higher purpose of serving God.[11] But this holds true only when that is what we're striving for.[12]

Shabbat is a weekly reminder of our call to holiness – to live for our ideals.

Chapter Notes

1. Genesis 12:1

2. Rashi, Genesis 12:2, based on Midrash, Bereishit Rabba 39:11

3. Genesis 12:2; Midrash, Bereishit Rabba 39:11; Rashi, Genesis 12:2

4. Genesis 12:1

5. Rashi, Genesis 12:1, based on Talmud, Rosh Hashana 16b and Midrash, Tanchuma, Lech Lecha 3

6. The ideas in this chapter are drawn from Rabbi Yaakov Krantz, the Dubno Maggid, Ohel Yaakov, Lech Lecha, Genesis 12:1, s.v. *v'hinei* et seq., based on Midrash, Yalkut Shimoni on the Torah 63.

7. Pirkei Avot 5:4

8. See Sforno, Deuteronomy 32:15.

9. Exodus 20:8

10. Talmud, Beitza 15b

11. Talmud, Pesachim 50b; Talmud, Nazir 23b; Talmud, Sota 22b, 47a; Talmud, Sanhedrin 105b; Talmud, Horayot 10b; Talmud, Arachin 16b

12. See Vilna Gaon, Even Sheleima 8:12, with the notes of Rabbi Shmuel Maltzen; Rabbi Eliyahu Dessler, Michtav M'Eliyahu Vol. 1, Teshuva, p. 24.

15 | Transcendent

Self-mastery is exhilarating. It empowers us to rise above our limitations. It is the key to cultivating good character as a whole, and the pathway to personal greatness. Shabbat – by the very fact that it is unmovable – helps us build the capacity to transcend the self.

Everything stops for Shabbat. No matter how important or urgent something may be, if it involves infringing the laws of Shabbat, we have to let it go. There's only one exception. As with almost all other mitzvahs, the laws of Shabbat are suspended to save a life.[1] Such is the sanctity of life that we are, in fact, *obligated* to break Shabbat to save a life, because the "laws of the Torah are not harsh – but bring compassion, kindness and peace to the world."[2]

This is a classic case of the exception proving the rule – Shabbat has absolute primacy.[3] Even the most sacred endeavors, such as the building of the Sanctuary, could not be carried out on Shabbat.[4] Nothing is more important. Not even making a living – to the extent that we are required to give up a job or close a business if it clashes with Shabbat.[5] On a more mundane level, if food for your meal was not cooked beforehand, or the lights were not switched on, you cannot do it on Shabbat.

This dedication to Shabbat requires profound strength, self-discipline, and faith. It requires, in a word, self-mastery. This means transcending our self-imposed limitations. When we feel the financial or social pressure to break Shabbat, and then rise above it, we achieve transcendence. Shabbat shows us that we can restrain ourselves and, in doing so, relinquish all the things we feel dependent on.

This is part of what makes Shabbat a holy day. Holiness means elevation above the physical.[6] It means that we are not bound by the needs of the body. We can transcend and direct our physicality in the direction of doing mitzvahs, building a family, making the world a better place. We can constrain these physical forces within us and make them serve us, rather than the other way around. We can harness our desire for pleasure, wealth, and honor to enhance our lives and our world rather than destroy and consume.[7]

This is the essence of free choice. The essential uniqueness of the human being is that we have the capacity to choose;[8] to override instincts in the cause of living a moral life. Animals are not capable of it.[9] This is what transcendence means. It is the capacity to master our inner life and not be subjugated by circumstances and the forces of human nature.

And that power of transcendence comes from the Divine soul within. We live in physical bodies and in a physical world, which are by definition limited. But God has given us a soul that can transcend the constraints of the material. We are not bound by our world – we can transcend it. In fact, on Shabbat, our ability to transcend is heightened; we are given an "extra soul"[10] – we are more attuned to the transcendent spiritual reality of existence; to our Divine values and to the true Master of the universe.

On Shabbat, we remind ourselves that God created the physical universe, and that therefore it is subject to His will. Once a week, when we grasp this fully, we rediscover the power He gave us to rise above the limitations of the physical world, to infuse our lives with meaning and purpose, and connect to eternity – to become transcendent.

1 As a rule, mitzvahs are suspended to save a life, Leviticus 18:5; Talmud, Yoma 85b; Talmud, Avoda Zara 27b, 54a; Midrash, Sifra, Acharei Mot 8:10; Rambam, Mishne Torah, Hilchot Yesodei HaTorah 5:1; Sefer HaChinuch, mitzvah 296; Shulchan Aruch, Y.D. 157:1. This also applies to Shabbat, Talmud, Shabbat 132a; Talmud, Yoma 84b; Rambam, Mishne Torah, Hilchot Shabbat 2:16; Shulchan Aruch, O.C. 329:1.

2 Rambam, Mishne Torah, Hilchot Shabbat 2:3, based on Leviticus 18:5. See also Proverbs 3:17; Talmud, Gittin 59b.

3 See Ramban, Exodus 20:8, based on Jerusalem Talmud, Nedarim 3:9, "The observance of Shabbat is equivalent to all other mitzvahs."

4 Talmud, Yevamot 6a; Talmud, Shevuot 15b; Midrash, Sifra, Kedoshim 7:7; Rashi, Leviticus 19:30; Rambam, Mishne Torah, Hilchot Beit HaBechira 1:12

5 The halacha requires us to forfeit all of our wealth rather than transgress a negative commandment. See Rema, O.C. 656:1, Y.D. 157:1.

6 See Rashi, Leviticus 19:2; Ramban, Leviticus 19:2.

7 See Chapter 24 below.

8 Derech Hashem 2:1:3. See also Pirkei Avot 3:19, based on Deuteronomy 30:15; Rambam, Mishne Torah, Hilchot Teshuva 5:1.

9 Rambam, Guide for the Perplexed, Part 3:17; Akeidat Yitzchak 8:3; Derech Hashem 2:1:3

10 See Chapter 3 above, note 31.

PERSPECTIVES

16 | Perspectives

Like character, our perspectives shape who we are. We have just explored how Shabbat nurtures within us virtuous character traits. In this part of the book, we explore some of the perspectives on our lives and our world that Shabbat teaches us.

How we view our purpose and role in life affects everything we do, feel and think. How we view our identity as Jews directly impacts how we express it. There are foundational truths that frame our philosophy on life and its meaning. Shabbat teaches us many of these ideas and principles that shape how we see the world.

These perspectives are embedded deep in our very being. Before our soul is sent down from up on high and placed into a body, we have absolute clarity.[1] We know what is true and what is right. We know our purpose. But then, once we arrive here, and enter our body, that clarity becomes clouded.[2] We can so easily lose our clear sense of purpose and identity. We need to remember the truths we once knew. Memory, in its most profound sense, is about rediscovering our essence – remembering who we *really* are and why we were sent here.

Our sages describe our earthly existence as the "world of forgetting."[3] We are surrounded by so many distractions that can lead us to forget the purpose of life. We live in a physical body, and in a physical world that can easily distract us with its glittering objects and enticing, though transient, experiences, and with the demands it places on us simply to survive. How do we remember why we were sent here in the first place? How do we remember that we are essentially a soul clothed in a body? How do we realign our perspectives with our true purpose?

Shabbat is a day of spiritual memory, of reorienting our perspective. "Remember the day of Shabbat to make it holy."[4] What does "remember" mean here? Clearly, it is something more profound than merely the act of mental recall. Shabbat is a day we remember who we are, where we come from and what our true purpose is.[5] It is the day set aside by God to illuminate our lives with Divine perspective, to activate our national memory of our birth at Sinai, where God gave us the Torah on Shabbat itself.[6]

The soul has absolute clarity. The body introduces murkiness and confusion. It is only at the moment of death – with the separation of the soul from the body – that a person rediscovers complete clarity. When we die, our soul leaves this physical world and we return to God and the world of the souls, and then we see again with complete clarity what the purpose of our lives was meant to be.[7] The moment we leave our bodies behind, we remember all the truths we understood so clearly before we were born. But while we are here, it is so easy to forget.

That is why it is a great kindness that God gave us Shabbat – a day for remembering and recalibrating, for reconnecting with the foundational truths of our existence. It gives us a glimpse of the spiritual clarity the soul gains after it leaves this world, which may explain why the sages of the Talmud describe the day as "a taste of the World to Come."[8] Shabbat is our lifeline to truth, saving us from being lost in a world of distraction. It is the day we transcend "the world of forgetting" and gain the Divine perspectives we need for life.

In the 15 chapters that follow, we explore 15 perspectives that Shabbat gives us, drawing on the teachings and insights of our great sages from across the generations. These perspectives lay the philosophical foundations of who we are, why we exist and what we are here to do. They are not merely abstract intellectual concepts; they are the foundational truths that animate our existence, coloring every moment of life with meaning and purpose.

Chapter Notes

[1]   The ideas in this chapter are drawn from Rabbi Yehuda Aryeh Leib Alter, the Sfat Emet, Shemot, Yitro 5662, Exodus 20:8.

[2]   Talmud, Nidda 30b

[3]   Sfat Emet, ibid

[4]   Exodus 20:8

[5]   The Sfat Emet points out that all the mitzvahs of the Torah serve to remind us of our mission in this world. There are two categories of mitzvahs – those that require us to do specific actions, reminding us that we were created to fulfill the will of God, and showing us how to do so, and those that require us not to do specific actions, reminding us not to get distracted by the temptations of the material world.

[6]   Talmud, Shabbat 86b

[7]   See Ramban, Torat HaAdam, Shaar HaGemul; Sefer HaIkkarim 4:33.

[8]   Talmud, Berachot 57b. See Chapter 25 below, note 2

17 | We Have a Creator and He Cares About Us

"You are my witnesses, says God."[1] Just as a witness is called to testify in court, the Midrash[2] says we have a sacred duty to testify to the foundational truths of the world in the court of public opinion – and especially to ourselves, our families and our communities.

We fulfill this duty when we keep Shabbat.[3] By doing so, we bear witness to the two foundational facts of our existence: that God created the universe[4] and that He liberated us from Egyptian slavery.[5]

We are literally God's witnesses to these facts because of our history as a people.[6] We witnessed, first-hand, God's awesome miracles to free us from Egypt, which has been reaffirmed in Jewish homes on the night of the Pesach Seder every year since the Exodus took place more than 3,300 years ago.

Our historical memory of the Exodus lays the foundation for our faith in God, because only the sole Creator of the universe could have such complete authority over nature as to change its laws at will – splitting seas[7] and turning rivers into blood,[8] alongside all the other miraculous plagues.[9] In other words, our belief in God as the Creator of the world is intertwined with our belief in God as the One who freed us from slavery. These truths are two parts of one whole and cannot be separated.[10]

We see this at the dramatic moment when God introduced Himself to the Jewish People at Sinai: "I am the Lord your God Who has taken you out of Egypt, from the house of slavery."[11] What's unexpected here is that God does not present Himself as the One Who created the world in the first place.[12] Surely, the fact that He took us out of Egypt is secondary to the fact that He created the world?

And yet, God introduces Himself as He Who broke the bonds of our slavery, because that is something we witnessed with our own eyes and experienced personally.[13] The generation that stood at Sinai had, just weeks before, witnessed the ten plagues and the splitting of the sea, among other miracles, and they encountered God through those experiences. That generation relayed their dramatic experiences to the succeeding generation born in the desert, who in turn relayed it to the generation that succeeded them – and so on, throughout Jewish history.[14]

Shabbat is a weekly experience of reaffirming these truths, and instills in us a faith in the authenticity of the origin story of the Jewish People – the very bedrock of our identity. The Divine origins of the universe and of the Jewish People are not just theoretical facts; they shape how we live, and determine our goals, priorities, and values. They give our lives meaning and purpose.

This is reflected in the rousing, ancient words of Kiddush, which we recite as we gather around our Shabbat tables. During Kiddush we testify that God created the universe and that He freed us from Egypt; we declare our loyalty to these truths and to our sacred mission that flows from them.[15]

When we affirm that God created the world, we testify that the beauty and engineering brilliance of the universe is His work, and acknowledge that existence is not the product of a random accident, of molecules colliding haphazardly.[16] Rather, it is the purposeful creation of an awesome Being beyond our comprehension. And when we testify that God freed us from Egypt, we affirm that God is deeply invested in human affairs; that He guides history, cares about us and watches over us, and that he gave us a mission to live by.

When we keep Shabbat, we relay these testimonies to our children[17] so that they, too, become God's witnesses – and so that one day, they will relay them to their own children, as each succeeding generation is entrusted with these foundational truths.

Chapter Notes

1. Isaiah 43:10, 43:12

2. Midrash, Vayikra Rabba 6:1

3. Midrash, Mechilta D'Rabbi Yishmael 20:14; Midrash, Lekach Tov, Exodus 20:13-14; see also Rabbi S.R. Hirsch, Genesis 2:1-3, Exodus 20:8-11, Deuteronomy 5:12-15, and Horeb, p. 62 et seq.

4. Exodus 20:11

5. Deuteronomy 5:15

6. The significance of the experience of the Exodus from Egypt as confirmation of God's creation of the world is explained by Rabbi Meir Simchah HaKohen, Meshech Chochmah, Deuteronomy 5:15.

7. Exodus 14:21-22

8. Ohr HaChaim on Exodus 7:22; See also: Exodus 7:20, with Bechor Shor and Chizkuni; Exodus 7:22, with Ibn Ezra, Rabbeinu Bechaye, Daat Zekeinim

9. Exodus 7-10, 12

10. The Rambam, in Guide for the Perplexed 2:31, explains that there are two facets to Shabbat: we rest to testify that God created the world and also to acknowledge that we owe our freedom to God, Who liberated us from slavery.

11. Exodus 20:2; Deuteronomy 5:6

12. Ramban, Exodus 20:2

13. Ibn Ezra, Exodus 20:1; Ramban, Exodus 20:2, 13:16, Deuteronomy 5:15; Rabbeinu Bechaye, Exodus 20:2; Kuzari 1:31; Tur, O.C. 271

14. Ramban, Deuteronomy 4:9; Sefer HaIkkarim, Maamar 3, 22

15. Talmud, Shabbat 119b; Talmud, Pesachim 117b

16. See Psalms 104:24; Rambam, Mishne Torah, Hilchot Yesodei HaTorah 2:2.

17. Ramban, Exodus 23:12. See Rabbi Moshe Feinstein, Darash Moshe, Parshat Tazria, Leviticus 12:2, that one reason we circumcise our sons on the eighth day, and not before, is so they first experience at least one Shabbat, which establishes the foundation of our faith.

18 | God is Holding It All Together

We see a world of disparate elements pulling in opposite directions: light and darkness, cold and warmth, summer and winter. We see the awesome detail and magical array of plant and animal life, living amid the vast rivers, oceans and mountains, and the great steppes and savannas. The complexity and brilliance are dwarfed by the pinnacle of Creation – the human being. The intricacy and diversity of our world is bewildering and dazzling. What holds it all together?

God is the grand unifying force of existence; He alone gives it coherence and harmony. One of God's names is Shalom[1] – peace – because He brings balance and harmony to the vastly disparate elements of the universe.[2] This idea is beautifully captured in a phrase from the Rosh Hashana prayers, proclaiming, simply, that God "holds it all together."[3]

In truth, this intrinsic unity of existence is not so simple. There is a constant struggle between the forces of harmony and coherence, on the one hand, and chaos and fragmentation, on the other. The Torah describes the state of the universe before the six days of Creation as "void and chaos, and darkness over the abyss."[4] We know that one of the cardinal principles of the Torah is that God created the world from nothing, and that He created everything.[5] This means – and the Midrash[6] states this explicitly – God actually created the chaos, void, and darkness; that the forces of fragmentation are essential elements of the universe.[7]

Shabbat is the counterforce to fragmentation.[8] The Midrash tells us that the chaos that existed before the creation of our world did not dissipate until God created Shabbat.[9] It compares the newly created world to an array of beautifully crafted utensils in a bath of frothy, bubbling water; only when the water clears can one discern and appreciate the beauty of the utensils. Shabbat cleared the chaos and anarchy that mired Creation at its outset, thereby enabling God's exquisite universe to be seen in all its splendor – as one beautiful, integrated, unified whole.

The Midrash also says that after God created the world, the universe continued to expand: heaven and earth stretched further and further away from the center, until God "pulled everything back."[10] The universe is, both literally and figuratively, expanding all the time; it is constantly in flux, moving in all different directions. And Shabbat is what draws the world back to its Divine center.

Shabbat brings harmony by returning the world to its Source, by reminding us that all of the remarkable diversity in the universe is the work of the One Creator.[11] When we keep Shabbat by suspending all creative activity, and when we recite Kiddush, we acknowledge God as the singular Creator of the universe, thereby reaffirming the ultimate unity of all of existence. Belief in one God – monotheism – is a foundation of being a Jew,[12] as the famous words of the Shema attest: "Hear Israel, the Lord is our God, the Lord is One."[13] God's essential Oneness has profound, far-reaching implications. It means that He is the one and only source of all things that exist, and the unifying force that holds everything together.[14]

Unity is the opposite of chaos. Chaos scatters everything in different directions, while unity signifies a coherent whole. Shabbat presents an integrated picture of reality, gathering a fragmented universe into one whole. It teaches us that we are held together by the ultimate unifying force of this universe – God, Himself.

Chapter Notes

1 Talmud, Shabbat 10b, based on Judges 6:24, "Gideon built an altar to God and called it 'God is Peace'"; Tractate Derech Eretz Zutta, Peace 11; Shulchan Aruch, O.C. 84:1, 89:2; Mishna Berura 84:6

2 Maharal, Netivot Olam, Netiv HaShalom 1:7

3 The Rosh Hashana Machzor, Mussaf, First Day, Kedusha

4 Genesis 1:2. Our translation of the word "*tohu*" as "void" is based on Targum Onkelos and Ibn Ezra and of the word "*bohu*" as "chaos" is based on Midrash, Bereishit Rabba 2:4 and Midrash, Pesikta Rabbati 33:1.

5 Rambam, Peirush HaMishnayot, Sanhedrin 10:1, Principle of Faith 1

6 Midrash, Bereishit Rabba 1:9

7 See Rabbi Yosef Dov Soloveitchik Halachic Man, Part 2, Chapter 1, p. 101 et seq., who explains the above Midrash in this way.

8 The idea presented in this chapter, that Shabbat is the counterforce to chaos, is drawn from Rabbi Shmuel Bornsztain, the Sochatchover Rebbe, Shem MiShmuel, 5671 Genesis 1:2-3.

9 Midrash, Bereishit Rabba 10:2

10 Midrash, Bereishit Rabba 5:8

11 See Isaiah 45:7.

12 Rambam, Mishna, Sanhedrin 10:1, Principle of Faith 2

13 Deuteronomy 6:4

14 Rambam, Mishne Torah, Hilchot Yesodei HaTorah 1:1-4

19 | God Elevates and Sustains Existence

Physical objects have six dimensions – up, down, left, right, forwards and backwards.[1] Think of a cube and these six dimensions become clear. But reality has a seventh dimension – the spiritual. In a cube this is represented as the center point from which the other six emerge. It is an intangible point, symbolizing the world that cannot be seen, but which is nevertheless foundational.

That is why Shabbat is the seventh day. It brings the spiritual dimension to existence. The number seven is the bridge between the physical and spiritual dimensions. It has elements of both. The world was created in six days, representing the six dimensions of the physical world. Shabbat is the seventh day – it exists in this world, and connects it to a different, higher dimension. The number eight represents another world altogether – a world that is purely spiritual. To summarize: six represents the physical. Eight represents the spiritual. And seven is the bridge.

After the six days of Creation, the world appeared to be merely a physical entity. It comprised the six tangible dimensions of reality and nothing more. And then, on the seventh day, God created Shabbat, and with it, birthed the seventh dimension into existence. Suddenly, reality was infused with a new dimension – with God's presence. Shabbat connects the physical world to the Divine, making the seventh dimension a part of our lived-in experience. It transforms our existence, connecting our world with its Creator.

God's presence brings two things to our world: elevation and blessing. He elevates physical creation with meaning, purpose and holiness. He also generates blessing, because He is the source of all life and energy and abundance.

Shabbat reflects these two aspects of God's connection with the world. The sages of the Talmud would welcome in Shabbat by invoking the image of Shabbat as a bride and a queen.[2] The Shabbat "queen" symbolizes the majesty and holiness with which God elevates our existence. The Shabbat "bride" symbolizes God's loving presence that brings blessing and abundance into our lives.

These two aspects – elevation and blessing – are reflected in the dual nature of Shabbat. It is a day of holiness and restriction – a day on which we refrain from many activities in acknowledgement of the sanctity of the experience. But it is also a day of blessing and abundance – a day we are commanded to celebrate, indulging in the wondrous bounty of creation.

This duality of Shabbat reflects God's twofold relationship with our world. On the one hand, He is the lofty and awesome King of all kings,[3] an all-powerful,[4] unknowable[5] Being. On the other hand, He is our loving Parent,[6] an intensely personal God, and the source of all life.[7] He is both immanent and transcendent, near us and beyond us, within us and above us.[8]

Through this dual relationship, God transforms our reality, elevating the world with grandeur and meaning, and blessing the world with warmth and kindness. Shabbat both reflects and enables us to embrace this duality. It is the bride and the queen. Linking the Divine with the earthly, the seventh day is the bridge between six and eight, the touchpoint between heaven and earth.

1 The ideas in this chapter are based on Rabbi Yehuda Loew ben Betzalel, Maharal, Tiferet Yisrael, Chapter 40.

2 Talmud, Shabbat 119a; Midrash, Bereishit Rabba 10:9

3 Deuteronomy 10:17; Proverbs 21:1; Mishna, Sanhedrin 4:5; Pirkei Avot 3:1, 4:29; Talmud, Sanhedrin 38a. On Friday nights when we sing "Shalom Aleichem," we refer to God as the "King of Kings."

4 Genesis 18:14; Deuteronomy 10:17; Jeremiah 10:7-9, 12; Psalms 94:9-11, 147:5; Daniel 4:31-34; Nehemiah 9:6; Job 36:21-22; Rambam, Mishna, Sanhedrin 10:1, Principle of Faith 1

5 Rambam, Mishne Torah, Hilchot Yesodei HaTorah 1:10; see also Isaiah 55:8-9.

6 Exodus 4:22; Deuteronomy 14:1; Pirkei Avot 3:18; Ruach Chaim, 2:1; Pirkei Moed, Rosh Hashana, Avinu Malkeinu, quoting the Ruach Chaim, 2:1. see also Rinat Yitzchak on Nefesh HaChaim 1:16.

7 Psalms 36:10

8 For God's immanence see: Numbers 14:21; Isaiah 6:3; Psalms 148:13; Talmud, Berachot 10a; for God's transcendence see: Isaiah 55:8-9; Ezekiel 3:12; Job 11:7; Talmud, Chagiga 13b.

20 | God is Close

What does it mean that God "rested" on the seventh day of Creation?[1] It is inconceivable that God requires rest.[2] And is it even possible that God ceased creating at the end of the first week of Creation, and on every Shabbat since then? This would seem to contradict what we say in our morning prayers: that the Creator, "in His goodness, renews, each day, constantly, the work of creation"[3] – that without His constant creative energy, the universe would cease to exist.[4]

The answers to these questions can be found in a deeper perspective of how God engages with this world.[5] We use human terms to describe the Divine, even though He is beyond such descriptions,[6] so that we have a way of relating to God.[7] With that caveat, we can think of God's creative interaction with the universe in three ways: thought, speech and action.[8]

During the six days of Creation, God brought the world into being with speech and action. On the seventh day, when it says that God "rested," it means that He ceased creating and sustaining the universe through speech and action, and instead created and sustained our world solely through His "thought."

Of course, there is nothing more essential to creativity than thought. On Shabbat, God continues to sustain the world through His creative energy, but does so with the closest form of that energy to Himself – His power of thought. On Shabbat, "all of the worlds are elevated"[9] – God draws closer to the world through the intimacy of His thinking, thereby infusing creation with Divine energy, holiness and light.

We pattern our behavior on God's own engagement with the world. Like the Divine, when we rest on Shabbat, we enter the sacred world of thought. We devote our minds to the rarefied world of Torah study. We feel an intimate sense of closeness with God on Shabbat as we return to our source.

The root of the word Shabbat is related to the word return. On Shabbat, the entire universe returns to its source. Before Creation, there was only God and the world of thought. In creating the universe, God transformed the world of thought into a world of speech and action. On Shabbat, when God's powers of creativity return to the level of thought, the universe returns to its Divine, pre-Genesis essence.

That is why, according to the Midrash, Shabbat is also a day of repentance,[10] which is about returning to our Godly essence. On Shabbat, like the universe, we return to our source, aided by our ability to reconnect with an extra dimension of our soul.[11] This reflects the deep spiritual parallel between how God interacts with the universe and the soul interacts with the body.[12] Shabbat is a day of the world returning to God and the body returning to the soul.

On Shabbat, God is closer to us and the universe than at any other time in the week. We feel God's presence more immediately, and we reaffirm and refocus on our essential, spiritual self – our own, inner reflection of the Divine. On Shabbat, the universe returns to its Divine source and is transformed – and so are we.

Chapter Notes

1 Genesis 2:3; Exodus 20:11

2 Isaiah 40:28

3 The Siddur, weekday Shacharit, blessings of Shema

4 Tomer Devora 1:1

5 The ideas in this chapter are based on the discourses of Rabbi Shneur Zalman of Liadi, the Baal HaTanya, published by his grandson Rabbi Menachem Mendel Schneerson, the Tzemach Tzedek, in Torah Ohr V'Likutei Torah, Sefer Shemot 3.

6 We use anthropomorphic terms to describe God but all of these are merely ways for us to understand Him; He has no physical attributes and is completely incorporeal. See Rambam, Mishna, Sanhedrin 10:1, Principle of Faith 3; Rambam, Mishne Torah, Hilchot Yesodei HaTorah 1:8-12, based on Deuteronomy 4:15; Hilchot Teshuva 3:7.

7 The sages explain that sometimes the Torah uses phraseology not to be understood literally but that best conveys the meaning of a subject. See Midrash, Mechilta D'Rabbi Yishmael 19:16, 19:18, 19:19; Midrash, Tehillim 1:3; Midrash, Lekach Tov, Exodus 19:18; Rashi, Exodus 19:18, 31:17; Rashi, Isaiah 63:1; Rashi, Talmud, Makkot 12a.

8 Zohar 3:83a, 3:229a; Zohar Chadash, Yitro 170; Eitz Chaim 47:2

9 Eitz Chaim 40:15

10 Midrash, Bereishit Rabba 22:13; Midrash, Vayikra Rabba 10:5; Midrash, Pirkei D'Rabbi Eliezer 19:3; Midrash, Pesikta D'Rav Kahana 24:11. See also Chapter 13 above.

11 See Chapter 3 above, note 31, for what this means.

12 Talmud, Berachot 10a; Midrash, Devarim Rabba 2:37. God is the hidden, holy lifeforce of the world, as is the soul to the body, and just as the world cannot survive a moment without that Divine sustaining energy, so, too, does the body die when the soul leaves it.

97

21 | **God Made Us a Nation**

Where do we come from? How did the Jewish People become a nation?

It all started with one family – the family of Abraham and Sarah, who, by the time their grandson Jacob and his extended family arrived in Egypt, numbered 70 souls.[1] But they were still individuals within a family. They were not yet a nation. God's vision was always for this family to become a nation with a historic Divine mission.

What was the exact moment the family of Abraham and Sarah became a nation? This is a critical question because the answer reveals the essence of Jewish identity. When announcing that He would liberate the Jews from the slavery and oppression of Egypt, God promised: "...and I will take you to become a nation to Me."[2] This, we know, was the ultimate goal of the Exodus.[3]

The verse implies that in Egypt they weren't yet a nation – they were simply a family of immigrants who grew to large numbers, were not accepted by their host nation and became victims of prejudice. They were a family of individuals held together by Divine promises and various cultural traditions, but actual nationhood was a promise for the future.

The Midrash[4] says that they retained their distinctive language, names and clothes that enabled them to be redeemed because they were identifiably different from the Egyptians. These cultural markers made the redemption possible, for without them there would not have been a distinct people to save; their assimilation into the Egyptian people would have been total. But these external trappings did not make them into a nation.[5]

The moment when everything changed – that a family became a people, that the Jewish nation was born – was at Mount Sinai.[6] There, the newly liberated slaves, the descendants of Abraham, Isaac and Jacob, accepted the Torah as their Divine and eternal mission, to be handed on to us, their descendants. In introducing that historic moment, God made it clear that Jewish nationhood and identity were bound up with His covenant;[7] that the moment a migrant family wandering the wilderness said: "We will do and we will hear"[8] was the moment when God fulfilled His promise: "...and I will take you to become a nation to Me."[9]

And the day it happened was Shabbat.[10]

It was on Shabbat that God revealed the Ten Commandments as the prelude to the entire Torah. We remember this every Shabbat, both through the prayers we recite recalling the Sinai revelation,[11] and through the call to "remember the day of Shabbat to sanctify it"[12] – referring to that day at Sinai when we received the mitzvah of Shabbat.

We were born as a nation on Shabbat. And every Shabbat – as we gather around the table with our families and recite the ancient words of Kiddush, the eternal Jewish mission statement, declaring that "You designated us and sanctified us from among the nations" – we remind ourselves who we are and what it means to be part of the Jewish nation. Shabbat reminds us that our origins and identity as a nation are like no other.

History has shown that nations are formed around shared land, language and culture; the product of various socio-economic, political, geographic, and other environmental factors. We are the only nation who was not formed by any of these factors – we were formed directly by God, charged with His values and mission.[13]

We were slaves in a foreign land, and then – after a miraculous, Divinely orchestrated liberation – we were born in a desert, on land belonging to no one. We are a nation because God designated us as such when He gave us the Torah as our founding constitution.[14] It was only 40 years later that, under God's mandate and Joshua's leadership, the Jewish People conquered the land of Canaan where they had originated, and made it the Land of Israel. Of course, the Land of Israel is a central focus of the Torah,[15] which makes it an important part of our national identity – but only because it is a platform to give expression to our Divine mission.

Reflecting on this, we understand that our identity as Jews is not only personal but national. The Torah and its mitzvahs guide our lives not only as individuals and families, but also direct us as a nation. There are mitzvahs directing the establishment of a fair judicial system,[16] an accountable system of government,[17] and the national-spiritual infrastructure of the Temple.[18] The Torah goes far beyond the realm of what is conventionally understood as religion, encompassing every field of human endeavor.[19] It is, indeed, a national constitution.

Grasping the essence of Jewish nationhood illuminates our past and our future. It solves the mystery of our survival. We are the only nation to have survived almost 2,000 years of exile intact. We have been scattered across the globe, separated from each other by vast distances, speaking different languages, living in different cultures, pursued and persecuted. And yet we are here to tell the story – the same people with the same values and vision as the Jews who were driven out of the land of Israel millennia ago.

There is no historical precedent for such a phenomenon. Our very existence is miraculous. By the normal laws of history, the Jewish People should be an ancient relic, confined to glass cases in museums, having disappeared like the other ancient nations – our contemporaries at the time we were born. Significantly, the ancient Roman Empire that sent us into exile has vanished without a trace, relegated to history books. Only we are left.

And the only way to make sense of this historical anomaly is to understand that we are a nation with a Divine mission. The miracle of Jewish survival is due to God's constant protection, enabling us to fulfill the sacred mission He gave us at Sinai.

Our great sages made bold predictions at a time when our future seemed so precarious. Pirkei Avot records the audacious claim of Rabbi Yochanan HaSandlar,[20] who – on the cusp of exile about 2,000 years ago, with the Land of Israel under Roman occupation and our situation seemingly hopeless – said that if we would remain "dedicated to Heaven" we would "endure forever."[21] How could he have known?

And then, 900 years later, Rabbi Saadia Gaon – who lived in what was then Babylonia under Islamic rule, when the Jewish People were centuries into a deep and seemingly unending exile, scattered and vulnerable – made the extraordinary assertion that we, "a nation only by virtue of the Torah," would last forever.[22] Who could have predicted then, more than 1,000 years ago, that we would be here today, alive and well, and learning and living the same Torah?

By understanding our past, we find direction for our future. Remaining loyal to our Divine mission is of strategic importance – it is the very secret of our supernatural survival. God has ensured we have survived and thrived against all odds to fulfill that mission. Jewish history has vindicated this. And every week, Shabbat reminds us of this foundational truth. It reminds us of the day we were born as a nation – "a nation only by virtue of the Torah."

Shabbat reminds us that Jewish nationhood is different from any other kind: that our national identity transcends time and circumstances, that we were born at the foot of a mountain in the middle of a desert, that our bonds of nationhood were forged not by man-made ideas or beliefs, but by Divine design – that we are a nation made by God.

Chapter Notes

1. Genesis 46:27; Exodus 1:5; Deuteronomy 10:22

2. Exodus 6:7

3. Numbers 15:41, as recited daily in the third paragraph of the Shema; Sefer HaChinuch, mitzvah 306. See also Exodus 3:12; Midrash, Tanchuma, Yitro 10:3.

4. Midrash, Vayikra Rabba 32:5; Midrash, Bamidbar Rabba 13:19-20; Midrash, Shir HaShirim Rabba 4:12; Midrash, Mechilta D'Rabbi Yishmael 12:6; Midrash, Pesikta D'Rav Kahana 11:6; Midrash, Tehillim 114:2

5. Maharal, Gevurot Hashem 43. See also Iggerot Moshe, O.C. 4:66 who says that these things referred to in the Midrash were only significant before the giving of the Torah when the Jewish People had nothing else to distinguish them from the Egyptians.

6. Talmud, Berachot 63b, based on Deuteronomy 27:9. See also Talmud, Yevamot 46b and Talmud, Keritot 9a that what happened at Mount Sinai was actually the mass conversion of the entire people to Judaism. In fact, the Talmud derives the laws and requirements of conversion from the process at Sinai, including, and most significantly, in terms of the theme of this chapter, the acceptance of duty to fulfill the mitzvahs.

7. Exodus 19:5-6

8. Exodus 24:7

9. Exodus 6:7, with Ibn Ezra, Ramban and Sforno; see also Maharal, Gevurot Hashem 43.

10. Talmud, Shabbat 86b

11. Shabbat Shacharit Amidah

12. Exodus 20:8

13. The ideas that appear in the next few paragraphs are drawn from across the writings of Rabbi S.R. Hirsch, most particularly from The Nineteen Letters. See letters 8 and16. See also his commentary to Exodus 6:7.

14. Rabbi S.R. Hirsch, Exodus 6:7

15. For examples see Genesis 17:8; Exodus 6:4; Leviticus 18:26-30; Numbers 34:1-15; Deuteronomy 11:12. See also Zechariah 2:16.

16. See Deuteronomy 16:18-20. See also Exodus 21-23.

17. For example see Rambam, Mishne Torah, Hilchot Melachim 5:2. See also Deuteronomy 17:14-20.

[18] For example see Mishna, Taanit 4:2.

[19] Rabbi S.R. Hirsch, Exodus 6:7

[20] Rabbi Yochanan HaSandlar (c135 – c170 CE) was born in Egypt (Jerusalem Talmud, Chagiga 3:1). He later moved to the Land of Israel where he became a student of Rabbi Akiva (Midrash, Bereishit Rabba 61:3, Kohelet Rabba 11:6). His devotion was such that even when Rabbi Akiva was imprisoned by the Romans, he found a way to secretly communicate with him about matters of Torah learning (see Jerusalem Talmud, Yevamot 12:5).

[21] Pirkei Avot 4:14, according to Machzor Vitry.

[22] Rav Saadia Gaon, Emunot V'Deot, Maamar 3, chapter 7

22 | Our Lives Have Purpose

Human beings are driven by a need to find purpose and meaning. And so, the most important question we can ask is: what is the purpose of life? The universe is dazzling in its complexity and beauty.[1] But why did God create it?[2] What, ultimately, did He want to achieve? And what is our role in His plan? The answers to these questions will guide how we live our lives.[3]

The starting point is to understand that God created two realities – physical and spiritual.[4] Both were created with "ten statements." God created the physical universe with the "ten statements" of Creation:[5] "let there be light"; "the earth shall sprout vegetation"; "the waters shall teem with living creatures"; and so on.[6] Similarly, when God revealed the spiritual underpinnings of the universe, He did so by means of the Ten Commandments, literally the "Ten Statements."[7] He used words to create worlds.

The ten statements of physical creation paved the way for the ten statements at Sinai. The ultimate purpose of the physical universe is as an arena in which to fulfill the precepts of the spiritual universe – the Torah and its commandments.[8] The spiritual universe is primary; the physical universe only has meaning and purpose insofar as it enables and gives expression to its spiritual counterpart.[9] Similarly, our bodies have meaning and purpose only in relation to our souls.

PERSPECTIVES

Shabbat allows us to see past the distractions of the material world to discover its hidden, spiritual underpinnings – to perceive the underlying Divine purpose of Creation. On Shabbat, the ten statements with which the physical world was created, recede. God stops creating and so do we – and so the physical world becomes less dominant, allowing the spiritual universe to come into view.

Shabbat is a day when we pull back from our own physical creative acts of dominance – the cacophony of human activity that can be so loud and unremitting that it drowns out who we are – in order to reveal the real purpose of Creation. This is the message of Shabbat – that the entire physical universe was created only as a place for the Torah to be fulfilled. It is no coincidence, therefore, that God first revealed the Torah on Shabbat.[10]

Similarly, Shabbat enables us to discover our own personal purpose, our sense of self. Like the universe, we too are a composite physical-spiritual makeup.[11] And when the commotion and overbearing physicality of the world recedes on Shabbat, our souls shine through; we feel more spiritual, more *human*. Shabbat is a "sign"[12] – our weekly reminder that God created the world with a purpose, and that our lives, too, are charged with Divine purpose: doing good through His commandments.

The spiritual clarity we receive on Shabbat is reflected in our faces. Unlike animals, no two human beings share the same face. The Talmud says that each person's unique face is an expression of a unique personality.[13] The face is the window to the soul, which is why, when a person dies and the soul departs, the face becomes ashen.[14] The unique glow of a human face – a reflection of the Divine essence of every human being – reflects the light of the soul. This spiritual light emerges with special intensity on Shabbat. The Midrash says that the sanctity of Shabbat is reflected in "the shining face of a person,"[15] and that "the light of a person's face on Shabbat is incomparably greater than during the week."[16]

When the world goes quiet on Shabbat, the soul comes to the fore. We become who we truly are. We remember that the body is only the vessel that enables the soul to express itself in this physical world. The unique spiritual light that shines from our unique face represents our unique spiritual mission in life. Shabbat transforms us into people with purpose, whose identity is spiritual.

This idea – that Shabbat gives us a "new face" – is dramatically illustrated by the laws of *sheva brachot*, the blessings we recite at a series of festive meals with the bride and groom in the week following their wedding (blessings also recited at the *chuppah*).[17] The *halacha* requires us to say these blessings only if there is a "new face" present – a person who was not at the wedding.[18]

But there is an exception to this rule – on Shabbat, we do not need a new person present in order to say the seven blessings. Shabbat itself brings a "new face" to each person present at the festivities.[19] Shabbat is different, and on Shabbat, *we* are different. On Shabbat we are all new people because it is the day the physical forces of the universe recede before the spiritual. We see each other and ourselves with a new light – the light of the soul.

Shabbat renews everyone at the table – we all have a "new face" because it is a day that our spiritual self radiates anew. Shabbat changes us. It gives us a "new face" by enabling the Divine light of our soul to shine through.

It reveals the Divine purpose of our lives and the Divine essence of our world.

Chapter Notes

1 See Psalms 104:24

2 See Derech Hashem 1:2.

3 The ideas in this chapter are based on the insights of Rabbi Yitzchak Hutner, Pachad Yitzchak, Shabbat, Maamar 1.

4 Talmud, Menachot 29b

5 Pirkei Avot 5:1

6 Genesis 1:3-31

7 Exodus 20:1-14; Deuteronomy 5:6-18. See Chapter 23 below.

8 Pirkei Avot 6:11, based on Isaiah 43:7; Talmud, Shabbat 88a; Talmud, Avoda Zara 3a, 5a; Midrash, Aggada, Genesis 1:1, Midrash, Lekach Tov, Genesis 1:1 and Song of Songs 5:11. All of the Midrashim are based on Proverbs 8:22 and Jeremiah 2:3. See also Rashi, Genesis 1:1; Derech Hashem, 1:2; Tanya, Ch. 36.

9 Pirkei Avot 4:21

10 Talmud, Shabbat 86b

11 Talmud, Berachot 10a; Derech Hashem 1:3:2

12 Exodus 31:17

13 Talmud, Berachot 58a

14 Tractate Kalla Rabbati 3:4

15 Midrash, Bereishit Rabba 11:2; Midrash, Mechilta D'Rabbi Yishmael 20:11

16 Midrash, Bereishit Rabba 11:2

17 Talmud, Ketubot 7b; Rambam, Mishne Torah, Hilchot Ishut 10:3; Shulchan Aruch, E.H. 62:1, 6

18 Talmud, Ketubot 7b; Rambam, Mishne Torah, Hilchot Berachot 2:10; Shulchan Aruch, E.H. 62:7

19 Tosafot on Ketubot 7b; Kol Bo 25:144; Teshuvot HaRosh 22:13; Rosh on Ketubot 1:13; Shulchan Aruch, E.H. 62:8

23 | Mitzvahs Connect Us to God and People

What makes the Ten Commandments[1] so important? We have 613 mitzvahs.[2] Why were these ten set apart from the rest of the Torah and given such attention?[3] And why were they the very first words that God chose to introduce Himself and His Torah to the Jewish People?[4]

The centrality of the Ten Commandments[5] is in how they establish the basic conceptual framework of all the mitzvahs: Creator and created, Commander and commanded, Source and subordinate. The word "mitzvah" means "commandment," which, by definition, entails a relationship between the commander and the one who is commanded. The root of the word 'mitzvah' means connection or attachment, reflecting how it bonds us with our Creator.[6]

The first five commandments relate to God – Creator, Commander, Source; the second five relate to people – created, commanded, subordinate. The first five represent the concept of the Commander and the second five represent the concept of the commanded – the two concepts together form the logical basis of the rest of the mitzvahs, which only make sense within the context of our relationship with God.[7] Hence, before the other commandments were given, the Ten Commandments set up the framework.

The starting point – the foundation of all foundations – is the first commandment: "I am the Lord your God." This is the belief that

God exists,[8] and that He is the source of all existence;[9] that He is the lifeforce of the universe without Whom nothing could exist, and that He is the one and *only* Supreme Being.[10] This leads us to the second commandment: "Do not have any other gods before Me." Respect and honor shape our relationship with Him, as is reflected in the third commandment: "Do not take the Name of the Lord your God in vain," while the fourth commandment – to keep Shabbat – is to testify to the fact that God is the Creator of our universe. By honoring our parents – the fifth commandment – we acknowledge them as God's co-creators in bringing us into the world;[11] that honoring them goes with honoring God.

The next five commandments govern our relationship with others, beginning with the duty to respect the Divine lifeforce within every human being: "Do not murder." Our obligation to honor one another is extended to the most sacred human bond of marriage: "Do not commit adultery."

"Do not steal," according to the Talmud,[12] refers to kidnapping – meaning we should respect and uphold human autonomy and freedom. We are then called on to inflict no harm on another – not even verbally, through false testimony, which includes respecting the legitimate legal rights of all people. And finally, our goodwill to others should even permeate our hearts as we strive to nurture a generosity of spirit that would preclude jealousy.

Shabbat is the connector between the first five and the second five because it establishes the bond between God and our world, reminding us that God created this world, and, most importantly, the people in it.[13] Our respect and care for others are predicated on this fact – as Pirkei Avot says: "Beloved is the human being created in God's image."[14] When the Ten Commandments instruct us to respect the life, marriage, freedom and possessions of other people, it is because we are all God's creations, and intimately connected with Him.

The intrinsic unity of the Ten Commandments, and hence the entire Torah system, is reflected in the Midrash[15] which says that when God gave us the Ten Commandments, He uttered them all "in one breath" – something beyond human experience or imagination. "In one breath" teaches us that the Torah system is holistic and integrated; our relationship with God cannot be separated from our relationship with people. We cannot respect the one and not the other.[16] We cannot be devoted to God and unethical in our dealings with people. Likewise, we cannot respect people and ignore God. It is one system.

Shabbat is the link that holds the system together because it reminds us that people are God's creations and hence deserving of respect just as He is. And it reminds us that if we disregard God, the very foundations of our morality crumble.

Ultimately, the mitzvahs were given to us to improve and develop ourselves, and fulfill our potential.[17] Even before beginning to explore how the mitzvahs enable us to grow as people, we need to grasp – and embrace – our relationship with the One who formulated them.[18]

This is what the Ten Commandments are about. With Shabbat at their heart, they lay the foundations of the entire system of mitzvahs – because they lay the foundations for our relationship with God.

Chapter Notes

1. Exodus 20:1-14; Deuteronomy 5:6-18

2. Talmud, Makkot 23b

3. See Talmud, Berachot 9b.

4. The following analysis of the Ten Commandments is based on the Maharal, Tiferet Yisrael 35-36.

5. As per the previous note, the approach taken in this chapter as to the centrality of the Ten Commandments is based on the Maharal. There are a number of sources that demonstrate how the Ten Commandments allude to and represent all the 613 commandments of the Torah: Jerusalem Talmud, Shekalim 6:1; Midrash, Bamidbar Rabba 13:15-16, 18:21; Midrash, Shir HaShirim Rabba 5:14; Midrash, Yalkut Shimoni on Torah 368, 825; Rashi, Exodus 24:12; Ramban, Kitvei HaRamban, Essay on The 613 Commandments derived from the Ten Commandments; Kuzari 1:87, 2:28.

6. The Aramaic root of the word mitzvah connotes closeness and relationship and so alludes to connection to God. For example, see Talmud, Bava Metzia 28a where the Aramaic word *tzavta* means to join or attach; Talmud, Bava Batra 80a; Talmud, Berachot 6b; Talmud, Sukka 52a (Ohr HaChaim, Exodus 27:20).

7. Mitzvahs can be divided into two broad categories – those between people and God, and those between one person and another. This explains why the Ten Commandments were written on two tablets – one for each category (Midrash, Mechilta D'Rabbi Yishmael 20:13).

8. Rambam, Sefer HaMitzvot, Positive Mitzvah 1; Sefer HaChinuch, mitzvah 25

9. Rambam, Mishne Torah, Hilchot Yesodei HaTorah 1:6

10. Rambam, Mishne Torah, Hilchot Yesodei HaTorah 1:3

11. Jerusalem Talmud, Kilayim 8:4; Talmud, Nidda 31a; Midrash, Sifra, Kedoshim 1:7

12. Talmud, Sanhedrin 86a

13. Maharal, Tiferet Yisrael 36

14. Pirkei Avot 3:18; see also Genesis 1:26-27, 9:6

15. Midrash, Bamidbar Rabba 11:7; Midrash, Mechilta D'Rabbi Yishmael 20:1, 20:8; Midrash, Aggada, Exodus 20:19

16. Reflections of the Rav, Vol. I, p. 193-195

[17] See Chapter 2 above, note 8, and Chapter 3 above.

[18] Rambam, Mishne Torah, Hilchot Yesodei HaTorah 1:1-6

24 | Our Mission is Broad

Rabbi Yitzchak Hutner was one of the great Torah scholars and thought leaders of the post-Holocaust era. A student once wrote to him, expressing discomfort that since leaving yeshiva and entering the working world, he had begun leading a "double life" – part religious, part secular; that his identity felt conflicted and disjointed.

Rabbi Hutner reassured his student with a metaphor:[1] if someone has a house, and in addition they then rent a hotel room, they are living a double life. But if that person has a house with two rooms, they are not living a double life, but rather a *broad* life. Rabbi Hutner told his student of a prominent doctor at Shaare Zedek Hospital in Jerusalem who would pray fervently with his patients before they went into surgery. The doctor saw his work of healing as part of his service of God. He didn't compartmentalize his life into "religious" and "secular" – everything he did was integrated into one holistic, coherent life, dedicated to Divine service.

"Let all of your actions be for the sake of Heaven" is how Pirkei Avot[2] crystallizes this way of living. This is not only an abstract philosophical idea; it gives us a practical guideline for life, which is so real that an entire chapter in Shulchan Aruch[3] gives concrete examples of what this means.

If we sleep and eat in order to have the energy to be productive – to make a contribution to the world, to help others and to do

God's will by fulfilling His commandments – then our sleeping and eating are transformed into mitzvahs.[4] Likewise, going to work or conducting business can be a mitzvah, depending on our intentions. If our intention is to earn a living in order to fulfill mitzvahs such as supporting one's family with dignity,[5] giving charity,[6] supporting Torah education,[7] providing people with jobs,[8] or even helping them indirectly through supporting the economy,[9] then that work itself becomes a mitzvah.[10]

Our calling is to live an integrated life, without split identities and compartmentalized values. It all depends on our mindset. If we view our lives holistically, we'll realize that everything we do can be part of our Divine mission, even those things that are not formal mitzvahs.

The Midrash gives an example of a righteous shoemaker who sews every stitch with the intention of helping people and sanctifying his work.[11] It is for this reason that certain rabbis of the Talmud were identified by their trade:[12] "Rabbi Yochanan the Shoemaker,"[13] for example, or "Rabbi Yitzchak the Blacksmith."[14] Their work was part of their mission.

Every aspect of our lives can be meaningful. If we dedicate ourselves to a higher purpose, every minute of our lives is a mitzvah. When we live with this holistic mindset, then the whole world becomes an arena for God-consciousness and for serving the Creator. Central to this worldview is that all of existence is one unified whole; everything is connected to one God, Who created it all,[15] a fact we remind ourselves of and celebrate on Shabbat.

As a total immersive experience, Shabbat teaches us that everything we do has mitzvah potential. On Shabbat, all our seemingly mundane activities – eating, sleeping, wearing fine clothes, drinking wine, singing, walking – become mitzvahs.[16] The day cloaks everything we do with sanctity and purpose. The

Talmud says that even the way we walk and talk should reflect the holiness of the day.[17]

These ideas of the broadness of our mission are expressed in how the Torah unexpectedly frames our weekday work as a Divine value, and even seems to equate it with keeping Shabbat: "Six days you shall work... and the seventh day is Shabbat."[18] The message is clear – our seemingly mundane weekday work can be holy, too.[19]

It goes further. We know that on Shabbat we refrain from the 39 categories of creative acts used to construct the Sanctuary.[20] So when the Torah juxtaposes "six days you shall work" with "you shall not work on the seventh day,"[21] it refers to the work that built the holy Sanctuary. By equating our weekday work with the building of the Sanctuary – and with God's own creation of the universe – the Torah implies that even seemingly mundane activities have Divine purpose. We create *our* world by transforming it into a place of meaning and Godliness.[22] This is the message of Shabbat and its definition of "work," as it teaches us how broad our mission is – and how we can transform the world into a sanctuary of meaning.

Chapter Notes

[1] Rabbi Hutner's response is published in Pachad Yitzchak, Igrot U'Ketavim no. 94, a collection of his letters and writings.

[2] Pirkei Avot 2:17. The Vilna Gaon ad loc. explains how this is derived from Proverbs 3:6, "In all your ways know Him..."

[3] Shulchan Aruch, O.C. 231

[4] Rambam, Mishne Torah, Hilchot Deot 3:2

[5] See Talmud Ketubot 47b, 50a.

[6] Deuteronomy 15:11; Talmud, Bava Metzia 31b; Rambam, Mishne Torah, Hilchot Matnot Aniyim 7:1; Shulchan Aruch, Y.D. 247-248

[7] Talmud, Bava Batra 21a; Rambam, Mishne Torah, Hilchot Talmud Torah 2:1, Hilchot Matnot Aniyim 10:16; Shulchan Aruch, Y.D. 245:7; Kuntres Hilchot Talmud Torah 1:3

[8] Talmud, Shabbat 63a; Rambam, Mishne Torah, Hilchot Matnot Aniyim 10:7; Shulchan Aruch, Y.D. 249:6

[9] See Mishna, Bava Metzia 4:12.

[10] Rambam, Mishne Torah, Hilchot Deot 3:2

[11] Michtav M'Eliyahu, Vol. 1, Kuntres HaChessed, quoting Midrash, Talpiot, 8, Chanoch.

[12] For deeper insights for these examples see Rabbi Avraham Grodzinski, Torat Avraham, Shabbat V'Aliya 6.

[13] First mentioned in Talmud, Berachot 22a

[14] First mentioned in Talmud, Berachot 41a

[15] Deuteronomy 6:4; Rambam, Mishna, Sanhedrin 10:1, Principle of Faith 2

[16] See Chapter 3 above and Chapter 35 below.

[17] See Chapter 3 above, notes 27-28.

[18] Exodus 20:9-10

[19] This idea is explained by Rabbeinu Bechaye in his commentary on the Torah, Exodus 20:9, quoting the Rambam, Guide for the Perplexed 3:51. See also Avot D'Rabbi Natan 11:1.

[20] See Chapter 3 above, note 6.

[21] Exodus 20:9-10

[22] Pachad Yitzchak, Shabbat, Maamar 6

25 | There is a World to Come

One of the most important truths of our existence is that there lies a world beyond this physical realm.[1] Our life in this world is only a temporary stage along the journey of the soul. Death is not the end. It is a transition to another state of existence – "the World to Come"[2] – a spiritual world, where souls live, eternally.

The Talmud describes Shabbat as a "taste of the World to Come."[3] Shabbat is a day that gives us a glimpse of the next world: closeness to God, an immersion in eternal values, profound peace, respite from the struggles of this world – a small taste of heaven on earth. Shabbat is a day of being and receiving – not dominating and imposing. On Shabbat, we see life not just through the narrow, constricted medium of our five senses, but with the heightened, spiritually attuned perspective of the World to Come. Shabbat reminds us that there's something beyond the world we can see. That there is, in fact, another world.

This perspective radically changes our outlook. Firstly, it gives us clarity on the purpose of life. As Pirkei Avot puts it: "This world is like a corridor before the World to Come; prepare yourself in the corridor so that you may enter the banquet hall."[4] This world has purpose only in relation to the next. We are here to prepare ourselves, grasping the opportunity to do mitzvahs, which can only be done with the body, here, in this world, as Pirkei Avot says further: "Better is one moment of repentance and good deeds in this world than the entire life of the World to Come."[5]

This world is the arena of action; where there is distraction, suffering, and temptation, and a body and soul combined into one being – created for the purpose of doing good by fulfilling God's will through His commandments. Only in this world do we have free choice, essential to the performance of the commandments;[6] it is the ability to choose to do the wrong thing that makes the choice to do the right thing meaningful.

When the soul leaves the body and ascends to the heavens, we no longer have that choice because that is a world of closeness to God and absolute moral clarity.[7] We remain who we are at the moment of leaving this world. We go to the 'World to Come' with whatever mitzvahs we have accumulated in this world.[8] That is why we prepare for the next world by doing mitzvahs in this one.

This teaches us to live with urgency and focus, and to treat our time as the precious, irreplaceable resource that it is. The Talmud compares this world to Friday,[9] and the World to Come to Shabbat.[10] We can only act and do mitzvahs in this world.[11] Not the next. Whatever we haven't done while we are alive remains undone forever. Similarly, on Friday, we try to finish all our work and utilize every moment; every second is precious as the clock ticks toward Shabbat. When the sun sets, we cease our work, and whatever is not done remains undone. If we haven't cooked before sundown on Friday, we will have nothing to eat on Shabbat.[12]

Shabbat teaches us to live life as if it is Friday afternoon, with sunset fast approaching – to live with a sense of urgency and an acute awareness of the preciousness of each minute. As Pirkei Avot teaches: "If not now, when?"[13] This approach to time forces us to be present in the moment and inspires us to use our time mindfully and wisely – knowing that every moment of life is sacred. [14]

But everything in this world is geared toward the eternal legacy of the next. Pirkei Avot[15] goes on to say: "Better is one moment of spiritual pleasure in the World to Come than the entire life of this world." All of the accumulated pleasures of this world do not compare to even one moment in the World to Come. This world was not designed as a place of tranquility and ease, a place to receive reward.[16] The World to Come is where we receive reward for all our efforts in this world – and where God ensures justice is ultimately done.

The two worlds are deeply connected to each other and, in terms of function and purpose, perfectly complement each other. Indeed, as both "a taste of the World to Come" and an undeniably earthy experience, Shabbat guides us to see them as one unified creation.

The Midrash[17] uses the analogy of a double-story palace to illustrate the relationship between this world and the next: God sees both levels, upper and lower, simultaneously, "in one glance." The secret to understanding life is contained in this phrase of the Midrash, "in one glance." God's "palace" comprises the lower world – the physical world we are familiar with, and the upper world – the spiritual world of souls.

We should not look at these two worlds in a disjointed way, disconnected from each other – they are two parts of one whole. We need to see them "in one glance" – as a single, two-tiered palace suffused with God's presence. Appreciating that this world and the next are part of one unified existence enables us to see the work of this world as preparing for the next.

It also gives us a vital perspective on suffering. If we view existence only through the prism of this world, the pain and apparent injustice will confound us. But if we see this world as part of a continuum, we understand that death is not the end, but the transition to eternal life. We begin to realize that the suffering of this world, while all too real and painful, is part of an eternal process that will ultimately reward those who now seem to struggle with undue suffering.

This does not mean that we can explain any *particular* situation of suffering.[18] According to the Talmud,[19] Moses asked God to help him understand the apparent injustices of our world – why it is that some righteous people suffer and some wicked people prosper, to which God answered: "No mortal can see Me and live."[20] In other words, only God knows why things happen in this world; to know why bad things happen to good people would be to know God Himself, which is, by definition, impossible. We cannot begin to understand God's ways.[21] If even Moses was troubled by this profound existential question, and God said that it is beyond human understanding, then it would be foolish to claim that we have the answers.

However, viewing the physical and spiritual worlds as one entity, while it does not answer questions related to specific tragedies, does provide context. We live in this physical world, but in the scheme of eternity, life does not end when our souls leave our bodies, life simply continues in another level of God's house. Our Divine tradition teaches us that a righteous person who suffered terribly in this world will receive great reward in the next; and a wicked person who may have prospered greatly in this world will be held accountable in the next.[22]

These ideas help us understand why Psalm 92, which contains no direct mention of Shabbat, is called the "Psalm of the Song for Shabbat." Shabbat is the day when God brought Creation to a state of completion and wholeness, where everything was finally in place. This psalm of Shabbat is a reflection of the day itself and celebrates what God has created, and so it confronts the difficulty of the suffering and the apparent injustices we see. The psalm describes how the wicked seem to "prosper like grass"[23] and the righteous are "like a cedar tree."[24] While it seems as though the wicked flourish, in the end, like grass, they wither away and leave no trace behind. The righteous, however, endure like grand cedar trees, with deep roots and strong branches, hardy enough to live on in the eternity of the next world.

This psalm teaches us to view this world through the eyes of eternity – to understand that good deeds are treasured and rewarded by God in a world of eternal bliss and closeness to Him. Its profound words capture the spirit of Shabbat, the day we remind ourselves, and celebrate, that we live in God's palace, which encompasses not only this world but also the World to Come. Shabbat is part of this world and the next – it is the bridge between the two. By guiding us to see this world in the context of the next, it provides us with clarity and purpose, comfort and perspective.

Chapter Notes

¹ Talmud, Menachot 29b

² The commentators differ regarding the Talmud's use of the term "World to Come." Some say it refers to the spiritual world into which the soul enters after death; others say it refers to the time of the final messianic redemption. The conflicting opinions agree that there is a world of the souls and also that there will be a final redemption, it's just a question of how to interpret the term. In this chapter, we give expression to the opinion of the Rambam (Mishne Torah, Hilchot Teshuva 8:2, 8:8) and the Kuzari (1:109) that the "World to Come" is the world into which souls enter after death. This is in accordance with Midrash, Tanchuma, Vayikra 8. In Chapter 27, we give expression to the opinion that the "World to Come" refers to the new reality that will emerge on earth with the coming of the Messiah and the Resurrection of the dead. This is the opinion of Rav Saadia Gaon, Emunot V'Deot, Maamar 9, chapter 6; Tosafot, Rosh Hashanah 16b, s.v. *l'yom hadin*; Ramban, Genesis 2:3, Leviticus 26:12; Raavad on Rambam, Hilchot Teshuva 8:8; Sefer HaIkkarim 4:31; Derech Hashem 1:3:11; Maharal (Tiferet Yisrael 10, 15, Ner Mitzvah, Vol. 2, 46; Netivot Olam, Netiv HaTorah 1:16 based on Proverbs 6:22, Netiv HaLashon 6:3, Netiv HaTeshuva 2:2).

³ Talmud, Berachot 57b

⁴ Pirkei Avot 4:21

⁵ Pirkei Avot 4:22

⁶ Pirkei Avot 3:19, based on Deuteronomy 30:15; Rambam, Mishne Torah, Hilchot Teshuva 5:1; Derech Hashem 1:3:1.

⁷ See Sfat Emet, Exodus, Yitro 5661, 5662, based on Exodus 20:8.

⁸ Pirkei Avot 6:9

⁹ Talmud, Avoda Zara 3a with Rashi. See Rashi, Pirkei Avot 1:14, 4:21. See Shelah, Aseret HaDibrot, Shabbat, Ner Mitzvah 12, who says explicitly that we should think about this on Friday.

¹⁰ Talmud, Berachot 57b; see also Midrash, Bereishit Rabba 17:5.

¹¹ Pirkei Avot 4:21

¹² Rashi, Pirkei Avot 4:16

¹³ Pirkei Avot 1:14

¹⁴ Talmud, Yevamot 85a; Midrash, Bereishit Rabba 14:9; Midrash, Devarim Rabba 2:37; Rambam, Mishne Torah, Hilchot Shabbat 2:18; Shulchan Aruch, O.C. 329:4

[15] Pirkei Avot 4:22

[16] Mishna, Peah 1:1; Talmud, Kiddushin 39b; Talmud, Chullin 142a; Rambam, Mishne Torah, Hilchot Teshuva 9:1

[17] Midrash, Bereishit Rabba 9:3

[18] Pirkei Avot 4:19

[19] Talmud, Berachot 7a

[20] Exodus 33:20

[21] Isaiah 55:9

[22] Onkelos, Deuteronomy 7:10; Avot D'Rabbi Natan 39:1; Jerusalem Talmud, Horayot 3:2, based on Ecclesiastes 8:14; Talmud, Eruvin 65a; Talmud, Yoma, 87b, based on Proverbs 18:5; Talmud, Sanhedrin 70a; Talmud, Horayot 10b, based on Ecclesiastes 8:14; Zohar 1:25b, 1:180b; Midrash, Tanchuma, Mishpatim 9:3, based on Psalms 92:8 and Ecclesiastes 4:5; Midrash, Tanchuma, Ki Tisa 27:11; Midrash, Pesikta Rabbati 23:1; Midrash, Tehillim; 7:19, 73:1, 94:2 ; Midrash, Aggada, Deuteronomy 7:10; Midrash, Lekach Tov, Deuteronomy 7:10

[23] Psalms 92:8

[24] Psalms 92:13

26 | We Live in the Past, Present, and Future

Shabbat is a day that creates a dynamic fusion of past, present, and future. It teaches us not to view the episodes of the past as dusty historical artifacts, but as animating and compelling aspects of our identity today – and of our vision for tomorrow.

On Shabbat, we revisit the creation of the world and our spiritual birth at Sinai,[1] and we look towards our future redemption. Shabbat evokes the beginning of history and its end, and the journey in between. It also encapsulates the holiness of our three primary festivals – Pesach, Shavuot and Sukkot – which are in turn linked to Creation, Revelation and Redemption. Shabbat weaves together these strands of time into a tapestry of meaning and beauty, eternity and destiny.

The three central Amidah prayers on Shabbat correspond to the three great historic events connected to the day:[2] the Friday night Amidah refers to the first Shabbat of Creation;[3] the Shabbat morning Amidah recalls the giving of the Torah at Sinai,[4] which took place on Shabbat;[5] and the Shabbat afternoon Amidah evokes the Final Redemption, the 'Shabbat' of history,[6] when God's presence will be manifest in the world, and faith, harmony, and wisdom will abound. These three historic events evoked in our Shabbat prayers also correspond to the three required meals of Shabbat[7] – Friday night dinner, Shabbat lunch, and the Shabbat afternoon "third meal."[8] This is unique to Shabbat (on Yom Tov, only two meals are required).[9]

PERSPECTIVES

The intersection of past, present and future on Shabbat goes further. The Midrash[10] draws the parallel between Shabbat and the three festivals – Pesach, Shavuot and Sukkot – each of which is, in turn, connected to the three key moments of history. The pattern of connection is exquisite.[11]

During the week, we are stuck in our own "Egypt" – mired in the slavery of the workplace, beholden to the demands of societies whose values are often not our own. On Pesach, God granted us the gift of physical and spiritual freedom, taking us out "in haste,"[12] and every Shabbat begins with that same gift of a dramatic transition to holiness and freedom. This parallels the first Shabbat of Creation; Adam and Eve were created on Friday[13] and entered Shabbat only hours after coming into existence.[14] It represents the power we have to lift ourselves out of the darkness – to become holy and close to God; to enter the sacred space of Shabbat and leave behind the world of confusion.

Then, on Shabbat morning, the energy changes. No longer making the stark break between the mundane and sacred, between darkness and light, our focus now is to make ourselves worthy of retaining the holiness and inspiration, and integrate it more deeply into ourselves. We shift towards developing ourselves using God's gifts of wisdom and goodness. Our prayers at this time recall God giving us the Torah – corresponding to the festival of Shavuot, the anniversary of the Sinai experience.[15]

Shavuot, literally "Weeks," refers to the weeks of preparation leading up to the festival as we make ourselves worthy of the Torah through the mitzvah of "counting the Omer."[16] During this time, we take the initiative, owning our spiritual journey and rising to the calling of our Divine mission, viewing the Torah as a Divine blueprint for the present and not a dusty document of the past.

Shavuot celebrates our ability to sustain a life of holiness. Of course, we all have momentary flashes of inspiration. Our challenge is to convert these isolated moments into something enduring. The Jewish People left Egypt on a spiritual high, having just witnessed the ten plagues and the splitting of the sea. But after that initial euphoria, could we sustain the feelings of awe and gratitude? There were ups and downs along the way. There were moments of victory and defeat. But the gift of the Torah ensured that even in the barrenness of the wilderness, we were able to sustain lives of spiritual inspiration.

Our late afternoon Shabbat prayers evoke our hopes and expectations for the fulfillment of the prophecies of a redeemed world. This corresponds with the festival of Sukkot, when we read and contemplate the prophetic visions of the Final Redemption.[17] We long for the time when the world will enter a prolonged era of Shabbat-like harmony, faith, and wisdom. And just as God's presence will be all-encompassing at the end of history, we fulfill the mitzvah of Sukkah with our entire bodies – the Sukkah, symbolizing God's presence as manifest in the "Clouds of Glory," envelops us.[18]

We now see how Shabbat encapsulates the three festivals: Pesach, the beginning of holiness; Shavuot, the sustaining of that holiness; and Sukkot, the Final Redemption, the culmination of history when holiness fills the entire world. We also see how the three festivals are, in turn, connected to the key moments of history – the Shabbat of Creation, the Shabbat of Revelation and the Shabbat of Redemption.

Shabbat teaches us to experience time as non-linear, transcending the simple measurable units of marking time that flows in a straight line.[19] It is a day when past, present, and future intersect, as we experience the Shabbat of Creation, of Sinai and of a world redeemed. Shabbat brings the past to life and animates our dreams for the future, illuminating our origins and guiding us to where we need to go.

Chapter Notes

[1] The Torah was given on Shabbat. See Talmud, Shabbat 86b.

[2] Tur, O.C. 292

[3] "You sanctified the seventh day for Your Name's sake as the purpose of the creation of heaven and earth." (Siddur) This refers to the verses in Genesis (2:1-3) that describe Shabbat as the culmination of the six days of Creation.

[4] "Let Moses rejoice at the gift of his portion — that You called him a faithful servant. A crown of glory You placed on his head when he stood before You on Mount Sinai. And he brought down the two tablets of stone, on which was engraved the observance of Shabbat." (Siddur)

[5] Talmud, Shabbat 86b

[6] "You are One and Your Name is One" (Siddur). This phrase is based on Zechariah 14:9, which refers to the time of the Final Redemption, when everyone will recognize God's presence and be fully aware of His Oneness.

[7] The obligation to enjoy three Shabbat meals is derived from the fact that the word "day" is mentioned three times when the Torah discusses the manna (Talmud, Shabbat 117b, based on Exodus 16:25). Rabbi Gedaliah Schorr, based on the Tur's idea that the three Amidah prayers of Shabbat correspond to the three great "Shabbat days," explains that the word "day" subtly refers to these three great "Shabbat days." (Ohr Gedalyahu, Parshat Bereishit, 7)

[8] Talmud, Shabbat 117b, based on Exodus 16:25; Rambam, Mishne Torah, Hilchot Shabbat 30:9; Shulchan Aruch, O.C. 291:1

[9] Tur, O.C. 529; Shulchan Aruch, O.C. 529:1; Mishna Berura 529:13

[10] Midrash, Mechilta D'Rabbi Yishmael 16:25

[11] See Ohr Gedalyahu, Parshat Beshalach, 5, where Rabbi Schorr expands on the previous idea and shows the patterns of connection that are explained in the next few paragraphs.

[12] Deuteronomy 16:3

[13] Genesis 1:26-31

[14] Talmud, Sanhedrin 38a

[15] Talmud, Pesachim 86b; see Magen Avraham, 494:1.

[16] Rambam, Sefer HaMitzvot, Positive Mitzvah 161; Sefer HaChinuch, mitzvah 306. Both are based on Leviticus 23:15.

17 Talmud, Megilla 31a states that on Sukkot we read the haftarah from Zechariah 14:1-21.

18 Talmud, Sukka 11b. See Shem MiShmuel, 5678 Sukkot 8.

19 The idea that time can be non-linear as explained in this paragraph is drawn from Rabbi Yosef Dov Soloveitchik in his article "Sacred and Profane."

27 | Humanity Has a Destination

History is not endless. We are headed to the destination of a redeemed world filled with blessing. One of the basic principles of our faith is belief in this final redemption for humanity[1] – in the assurance of an abundant, peaceful and Godly world heralded by the messianic era.

Human history, according to the Talmud, is modeled on the six days of Creation followed by Shabbat. Each day of Creation represents 1,000 years of history, with the seventh millennium of history being a Shabbat-like era of redemption for all of humankind,[2] when, as our prophets proclaim, "the world will be filled with the knowledge of God, as the waters cover the sea;"[3] a time when all conflict,[4] famine, and suffering will end.[5]

Every week, Shabbat gives us a "taste" of what it will be like to live in this redeemed world,[6] a world of harmony, suffused with wisdom and faith. As Shabbat redeems the days of the week, the messianic era redeems the preceding 6,000 years of human history.

The Talmud divides these 6,000 years into three distinct eras: the first two millennia are the "years of chaos"; the next two millennia are the "years of Torah"; and the final two millennia are the "years of potential redemption."[7]

The years of chaos predate the birth of Abraham, who championed belief in God and ethical living; they are characterized as chaotic because without Torah principles and morality, the world lacked direction, coherence, and purpose. The years of Torah begin with Abraham's influence on the world in the year 2000 from Creation,[8] encompass the Divine revelation and the giving of the Torah at Sinai, and culminate with the distillation and transcription of the Oral Torah (given by God at Sinai alongside the Written Torah)[9] in the form of the Mishna in around the year 4000 from Creation (240 CE).[10] We then entered the third era of history: the 2,000 years most appropriate for redemption,[11] during which time the messiah could arrive at any moment, but no later than 6,000 years.

The model of Creation – six days followed by Shabbat – is therefore the model for all of human history. In fact, each day of Creation corresponds to each of the six millennia of history.[12] Shabbat is not just a day that affects us as individuals, or even as communities; it provides the focal point around which time – and all of human history – revolves.

By establishing that humanity has a destination – that history in its current form of struggle and uncertainty is not endless – God gives our world purpose. History isn't an aimless meandering – it is a purposeful journey toward an end point, a glorious culmination in which humanity finally attains the values of Shabbat in their fullest expression. The values that will permeate the world when this great Shabbat of history finally arrives – a universal awareness and embrace of God's presence, Torah wisdom, peace, and kindness, among others – give us a vision to strive for in our as yet unredeemed world.[13]

The vision is also a supremely optimistic one.[14] By guaranteeing that history will culminate in an era of peace, faith, and wisdom, God gives us the strength to march through history with courage and hope. At the very earliest moments of creation, we read that God created light and darkness.[15] The Midrash says this "light and dark" refers to the actions of the righteous and the wicked, respectively.[16] Surprisingly, the Midrash[17] asks whether God prefers the light or the darkness, and answers by citing the verse: "He saw the light and it was good"[18] – meaning God prefers the deeds of the righteous. Shouldn't this be obvious?

A way to understand the Midrash's question is this:[19] will God leave history to chance, and let the forces of light and darkness battle for supremacy, with no predetermined outcome? To which the unequivocal answer is "no" – "He saw the light and it was good." Somehow, by the end of history, the forces of light will triumph. God is giving us a guarantee that He will never let the world disappear into the darkness of a moral abyss, into spiritual oblivion. In the end, He will ensure that light will prevail and history will culminate in the values of Shabbat.

Chapter Notes

1 Rambam, Mishna, Sanhedrin 10:1, Principle of Faith 12

2 Talmud, Sanhedrin 97a, based on Psalms 90:4, 92:1. See Ramban's explanation of Genesis 2:3. See also Talmud, Rosh Hashanah 31a; Talmud, Avoda Zara 9a.

3 Isaiah 11:9; Habakkuk 2:14

4 Isaiah 2:4

5 Rambam, Mishne Torah, Hilchot Melachim 12:5

6 Talmud, Berachot 57b. See note 2 in Chapter 25 that there are two interpretations of what the "World to Come" is; in this chapter we give expression to the opinion of the Ramban and others that the "World to Come" refers to the new reality that will emerge on earth with the coming of the Messiah and the Resurrection of the dead.

7 Talmud, Avoda Zara 9a; Talmud, Sanhedrin 97a

8 Abraham was born in 1948 from Creation (Midrash, Seder Olam Zutta 3). When he was 52 years old, in the year 2000, he began reaching out to people and spreading faith in God (Talmud, Avoda Zara 9a). That year was, in effect, the birth of Torah in the world.

9 Talmud, Yoma 28b; Midrash, Sifra, Bechukotai, 8:10

10 The Mishna, compiled by Rabbi Yehuda HaNasi, was published in 3978/218 CE (Seder HaDorot citing Rav Sherira Gaon in Sefer HaYuchsin; Kuzari 3:67; Rabbi Menachem Nochum Twersky, Maor Einayim, Chapters 12 and 24. Maor Einayim also cites the Raavad and the Tzeida LaDarech, who maintain that this took place in the year 3948/188 CE).

11 See Maharal, Netzach Yisrael 27, 42; Netivot Olam, Netiv HaShalom 1; Be'er HaGola, Chapter 4; Chidushei Aggadata, Shabbat 55b; Drasha for Shabbat HaGadol.

12 The Ramban, Genesis 2:3, elaborates at length on how each day of Creation corresponds to what happened in history in that particular millennium.

13 See Rambam, Mishne Torah, Hilchot Melachim 12:5 for a description of the messianic age.

14 See Chapter 11 above.

15 Genesis 1:3-5

16 Midrash, Bereishit Rabba 3:8; Midrash, Lekach Tov, Genesis 1:5

17 Midrash, Bereishit Rabba 2:5

[18] Genesis 1:4

[19] This interpretation of the Midrash is drawn from Rabbi Yosef Yehuda Leib Bloch, Shiurei Daat, Vol. 1, Shiur 9, p. 131 et seq.

28 | The World was Created for Me

Imagine the very first Shabbat of history.[1] Just one couple, husband and wife,[2] together with God. The Talmud says that God created Adam and Eve on the sixth day – after everything else had been created – so that they would begin their lives by entering immediately into Shabbat.[3]

On Shabbat, as we reaffirm God created the world and each one of us, we remember how precious we are to Him. As the Talmud says: "Every person is obliged to say, 'The world was created for me.'"[4] The Talmud learns this from the fact that God created all plant and animal species en masse, while human beings were created as just one being (only later divided into two).[5] The whole universe was worth being created even if just one human being existed to inhabit it.

To say "the world was created for me" is not a statement of arrogance, which is one of the most serious of all character flaws.[6] It is a declaration of how valued each one of us is to God. The context of the Talmud's statement: "A person is obliged to say..." is significant. It appears among the laws of criminal procedure, which guide judges on how to conduct a fair trial – including discouraging witnesses from lying and, thereby, committing perjury. The Talmud stipulates that the judges read out a declaration to the witnesses to inspire them to tell the truth in their testimony.[7] Included in that declaration is this statement that a person should say to themselves: "The world was created for me."[8]

The awareness of our importance to God can inspire us to do the right thing – in this case, to tell the truth, and in general, to strive for moral and spiritual greatness.[9] When we realize our self-worth, that "the world was created for me," we are moved to live by higher ideals, to live up to our lofty standing in the eyes of our Creator.

Becoming aware of our self-worth instills in us a sense of dignity that protects us from temptation and wrongdoing. And it can inspire us to achieve things we felt were beyond us. We see this idea expressed in the construction of the magnificent and intricate Sanctuary in the desert, built after the people left Egypt.[10] As former slaves of Pharaoh, accustomed only to hard labor, the Jewish People lacked the skills, artistry, and experience needed to build such an elaborate structure[11] – yet they came forward to try and achieve what God asked of them.[12] This courage came from self-belief, a conviction that they had within them the ability to rise to the occasion. It came, essentially, from their awareness of God's faith in *them*.

The Talmud[13] tells the story of one of the most famous converts in Jewish history, a Roman by the name of Onkelos, who later became a renowned Torah scholar.[14] Before he converted,[15] Onkelos held a lofty position within the Roman Empire. The Caesar,[16] who was his uncle, was upset about his conversion and repeatedly sent soldiers to bring Onkelos back to Rome. But on each occasion, after Onkelos had spoken with these soldiers, they were so taken with his words that they converted to Judaism.

What did Onkelos say to these soldiers that had this profound effect?

To one group, Onkelos spoke about the pillars of cloud and fire that God "held" for the Jewish People to guide them through the desert after they left Egypt.[17] He contrasted this with an earthly ruler for whom it would be beneath his dignity to hold a torch for anyone.

To another group, Onkelos explained the concept of a *mezuzah*, through which God, Himself, "stands guard" outside Jewish homes. He contrasted this with an earthly ruler whose servants guard his palace.

What moved the Roman officers so profoundly was the insight that God regards each one of us as precious and gives us His personal attention and focus. He cares for us collectively, as He did with the pillars of fire and cloud, and also as individuals, represented by the *mezuzah* outside each and every home. This Divine attention inspires us to become better people; to live a holy, more noble life and achieve great things.

On Shabbat, we remind ourselves that God would have created the entire universe even just for one of us. We cast our minds back to that very first Shabbat, at the dawn of creation, when everything was made ready – an entire world waiting to welcome the very first couple. We contemplate that we, too, can feel as special as Adam and Eve who were the sole focus of God's love, generosity, and expectations – that "the world was created for me." And then we recommit ourselves to living up to His belief in us.

Chapter Notes

[1] Genesis 2:2-3

[2] Zohar 2:167b; Ibn Ezra, Genesis 4:1; Radak, Genesis 4:1; Rabbeinu Bechaye, Genesis 4:1. In contrast, see Talmud, Sanhedrin 38b with Tosafot; Midrash, Bereishit Rabba 22:2; Zohar Chadash, Midrash Rut 379; Rashi, Genesis 4:1.

[3] Talmud, Sanhedrin 38a with Rashi

[4] Mishna, Sanhedrin 4:5 (Talmud, Sanhedrin 37a); Midrash, Tanna D'Vei Eliyahu Rabba 25:1

[5] Talmud, Berachot 61a

[6] Rambam, Mishne Torah, Hilchot Deot 2:3, based on Deuteronomy 8:14

[7] Mishna, Sanhedrin 4:5 (Talmud, Sanhedrin 37a)

[8] Talmud, Sanhedrin 37a, as per Rashi.

[9] Rabbi Chaim Shmuelevitz, Sichot Mussar, 28, citing Talmud, Sanhedrin 37a, as per Rashi.

[10] This example and its explanation are also drawn from Rabbi Shmuelevitz ibid.

[11] Ramban, Exodus 31:2

[12] See Exodus 36:5-7.

[13] Talmud, Avoda Zara 11a

[14] Onkelos was the author of an Aramaic Midrashic translation of the Torah; see Talmud, Megilla 3a.

[15] This example and its explanation as set out in the next few paragraphs is drawn from the writings of Rabbi Natan Tzvi Finkel, Ohr HaTzafun, Vol. 2, Article 18, p. 100-105.

[16] Titus, who destroyed the Temple in Jerusalem. See Talmud, Gittin 56b.

[17] Exodus 13:21

29 | We are Partners with God in Creation

We move in the same seven-day cycle within which God created the world.[1] By linking our six days of work to God's six days of Creation, and our rest on Shabbat to His rest on day seven,[2] the Torah is comparing us to God in His capacity as a Creator, conferring on us our core identity as God's co-creators.

The Talmud[3] captures this idea with a profoundly simple statement that we become God's "partner in creation" simply by reciting Kiddush on Friday night. With the words of Kiddush, we declare that we are keeping Shabbat as a holy day because God created the world in six days and rested on the seventh,[4] and we reaffirm our role as God's partner in creation. But what does this actually mean?

The Midrash[5] relates a debate between an officer of ancient Rome, Turnus Rufus,[6] and the great Jewish sage, Rabbi Akiva. Turnus Rufus asked Rabbi Akiva: "Whose acts are greater, those of man or of God?" This was a set-up. Turnus Rufus's intention was to question how the Torah could command circumcision:[7] If God had wanted newborn sons to be circumcised, the Roman officer reasoned, He would have created them that way. What right do we have to make an incision on a baby just eight days out of the womb?

In response, Rabbi Akiva placed stalks of wheat and a loaf of bread before Turnus Rufus and asked him which he preferred.

Turnus Rufus replied, as expected, that he preferred the loaf of bread. Rabbi Akiva pointed out that God made the stalks of wheat, while man made the loaf of bread.

Rabbi Akiva's message was that God created this world in a state of potential. God does not want us to just accept everything as it is; He wants us to improve it. He gives us wheat seeds, but it's we who plant, nurture, and harvest the stalks of wheat; it's human creativity and ingenuity that transform a small seed into delicious and nourishing food. We are not going against God's will – on the contrary, this is precisely His will. So, when God commands us to circumcise our newborn sons, He is inviting us to join Him in creation, by sanctifying the baby to complete His creation.

The two examples in their debate are significant. Making bread represents the human partnership with God in creating and developing the physical world. Circumcision, signifying the Divine covenant with the Jewish People,[8] represents our partnership with God in creating and developing our spirituality. The mitzvahs in general, and Shabbat in particular, are the means God has given us to develop our character and perspectives. For six days we are creative like God, doing whatever is necessary to improve the world and advance society.[9] On Shabbat, we create ourselves.

And then when Shabbat departs, as we make Havdalah, we rededicate ourselves to our role as God's partner in creating the world around us. On the very first Saturday night of history, as Shabbat came to an end, Adam invented fire, the Talmud tells us, by rubbing two stones together.[10] It was humankind's first technological breakthrough, providing heat and light, so vital for human survival in a natural world. This proved a pivotal moment, a landmark achievement that cleared the way for many more advances that make up the basic infrastructure on which civilization rests.

Every week, as we mark Shabbat's departure with Havdalah, we commemorate the invention of fire[11] by lighting a flame and benefiting from its illumination, as we recite a blessing of thanksgiving and praise to God, "Who creates the lights of the fire."[12] This moment symbolizes the return to the work of the week, because on Shabbat we are not allowed to light a fire.[13]

It is significant that the words of the blessing refer to God and not humankind. The invention of fire was a triumph of human ingenuity, and yet it is God Who created the human intellect and spirit, as well as the basic elements of the world that give birth to fire if harnessed correctly.[14]

God embedded all the potential for the creation of fire during the six days of Creation. The Talmud says that God intended to create fire, but decided, instead, to grant Adam the insight to create it himself.[15] The invention of fire thereby becomes richly symbolic. On the one hand, it shows the greatness of the human spirit – our innate ability to create and achieve wondrous things. By enabling human beings to create fire, God showed us that we can rise above the natural world and impose our will on it through ingenuity.[16] All other lifeforms are submerged in nature; they take the world as they find it. Only the human being, created with a Godly soul, has the Divine power to shape and direct the natural world. Alone among God's creations, we have the ability to unlock the world's potential. On the other hand, through the blessing we recite on fire at Havdalah, we humbly acknowledge God as the ultimate source of all human achievements – as we do by refraining from igniting fire on Shabbat itself.[17]

Shabbat is a day to remind ourselves that God has given us the extraordinary honor of being His partner in creating the world – and ourselves.

Chapter Notes

1 This deeper understanding of the idea that we rest on the seventh day as God does is explained by Rabbi Tzadok of Lublin, Pri Tzadik, Kedushat Shabbat 1.

2 Exodus 20:9

3 Talmud, Shabbat 119b

4 Genesis 1:31-2:3

5 Midrash, Tanchuma, Tazria 5:1

6 A senator and provincial governor of Judea, known as Quintus Tineius Rufus in Roman sources.

7 Genesis 17:10-12; Leviticus 12:3

8 Genesis 17:10-14.

9 See Rabbeinu Bechaye, Exodus 20:9, quoting the Rambam, Guide for the Perplexed 3:51.

10 Talmud, Pesachim 54a

11 Jerusalem Talmud, Berachot 8:5

12 Mishna, Berachot 8:5 (Talmud, Berachot 51b, 52b); Rambam, Mishne Torah, Hilchot Shabbat 29:24; Shulchan Aruch, O.C. 298

13 Taamei HaMinhagim, Kuntres Acharon 411

14 This concept is explained by Rabbi A.Y. Kook, Ein Ayah, Berachot 52b, note 1.

15 Talmud, Pesachim 54a

16 Maharal, Be'er HaGola 2:10

17 Exodus 35:3. See Chapter 5 above.

30 | Family is Everything

Gratitude is the oxygen of relationships. A bond of love and respect between people cannot survive if they do not feel and express gratitude to each other. Being grateful for the kindness and support of others is also about basic integrity. The home is the laboratory where we learn gratitude for the first time in relation to our parents.[1]

Gratitude begins with the mitzvah of honoring parents, which explains its connection with the mitzvah that often appears alongside it in the Torah – Shabbat.[2] Both mitzvahs are rooted in gratitude for the most basic of all gifts – life itself. We owe our lives to our parents – and to God, Who is also described in our sources as a parent.[3]

Both mitzvahs are about acknowledging our source of life.[4] On Shabbat, we proclaim God as the Creator of our world and of all existence.[5] And, of course, our parents are the ones who, in partnership with God, created us and brought us into this world – as the Talmud says: "There are three partners in the creation of a person."[6]

The juxtaposition of these relationships is significant. Ingratitude is not compartmentalized; it seeps from one relationship into another. If a person is ungrateful to their parents, it will also affect their relationship with God, which is founded on recognizing that everything we are and have is from Him – including our parents.

The mitzvah of Shabbat is about honoring the ultimate Creator Who created our parents in the first place. This explains why, if a parent instructs a child to break Shabbat, that instruction is null and void.[7] The mitzvah of honoring parents makes way for the even more foundational acknowledgement of our Creator, Who created everything and all people.

Honoring parents is also the secret to the endurance of the Jewish People. If children don't trust and respect their parents, the very transmission of the Torah is in jeopardy.[8] Thus, the mitzvah of honoring parents, founded on gratitude, has pride of place among the Ten Commandments, relayed by God Himself at Sinai.[9] The message is clear: the Divine mission we received at Sinai is dependent on the relationship between parents and children – on the strength of the Jewish family.

So much of the Shabbat experience revolves around family. The three meals are sacred moments to eat, sing, debate, discuss, and engage as a family.[10] At the Friday night Shabbat table, many have the custom to bless their children.[11] The Shabbat atmosphere as a whole lends itself to family bonding, and especially to building the connection between parents and children.

The family unit is the foundation of humanity. The whole of humankind stemmed from the family of Adam and Eve. Then, at the time of the flood, it was Noah and his wife, and their sons and wives, who formed the kernel of the new world that was built after the destruction. Similarly, the foundations of the Jewish People are the families of our founding fathers and mothers – Abraham and Sarah, Isaac and Rebecca, Jacob and Rachel and Leah.[12] Jewish history and destiny are intertwined with the fate of these families.

The very structure of the Jewish People – the delineation of the Twelve Tribes – is derived from the family of Jacob and his sons. It is for this reason that we are called the "House of Israel."[13] The

Jewish nation is essentially one large family made up of many subfamilies. We see this clearly expressed in the way the people were counted in the desert at certain key moments after the Exodus – the nation was delineated as a collection of families: twelve familial tribes, each comprising various familial branches.[14]

The family is the bedrock of the Jewish People. It is the source of transmitting our legacy as a people. And Shabbat plays a vital role in nurturing and strengthening the Jewish family.

Chapter Notes

[1] The idea of gratitude and the connection between honoring parents and God as expressed in the next few paragraphs are based on Sefer HaChinuch, mitzvah 33.

[2] Exodus 20:8-12; Leviticus 19:3; Deuteronomy 5:12-16

[3] Exodus 4:22; Numbers 11:12; Deuteronomy 1:31, 14:1, 8:5, 32:6; Isaiah 49:15, 64:7, 66:13; Psalms 89:27, 103:13; Mishna, Sota 9:15; Talmud, Berachot 35b; Zohar 3:82b; Midrash, Tanna D'vei Eliyahu Rabba 16:1; Midrash Tehillim 27:2

[4] This idea is drawn from Kli Yakar, Leviticus 19:3 and Deuteronomy 22:7, who also applies it to explain why the mitzvahs of sending away the mother bird before taking her chicks or eggs (*shiluach hakein*) and honoring parents are also linked in the Torah (Exodus 20:12, Deuteronomy 5:16, 22:7). Both are about honoring the source of life, our parents and the mother bird. This in turn reminds us that God is the ultimate source of life.

[5] Exodus 20:11

[6] Talmud, Kiddushin 30b; Talmud, Nidda 31a

[7] Talmud, Yevamot 5b, based on Leviticus 19:3. This principle is also applicable to other mitzvahs. See Talmud, Bava Metzia 32a; Rambam, Mishne Torah, Hilchot Mamrim 6:12; Shulchan Aruch, Y.D. 240:15.

[8] See Ramban, Deuteronomy 4:9.

[9] Rabbi S.R. Hirsch, Exodus 20:11; Meshech Chochmah, Leviticus 19:3

[10] See Chapter 3 above, notes 19 and 23.

[11] See Chapter 6 above, note 9.

[12] Rachel is mentioned before Leah as per Rashi, Genesis 31:4.

[13] Exodus 16:31, 40:38; Leviticus 10:6, 17:3, 17:8, 17:10, 22:18; Numbers 20:29; Joshua 21:45; Mishna, Yoma 6:2; Mishna, Nedarim 3:11; Mechilta D'Rabbi Yishmael 14:22; Midrash, Tanchuma Buber, Vayetzei 15:1

[14] The Torah records two censuses (Numbers 1 and 26). The first took place at the beginning of the Jewish People's 40 years in the desert after the construction of the Sanctuary (Numbers 1:1 with Rashi). The second took place towards the end of the 40 years after thousands had died in a plague (see Numbers 25:1-9).

31 | **We Build Community**

Community is created when people collaborate to create something together. When Moses led the people in building the Sanctuary in the desert, he "gathered together all the Children of Israel,"[1] forging them as a community for a collaborative project. They donated the building materials needed, each contributed a half-shekel silver coin, and some were directly involved in its construction. This was a truly communal project that the Jewish People as a whole were credited with.[2]

At the same moment that this sense of community was being formed through the collaboration on the Sanctuary, Moses taught them about Shabbat, another binding force of community. The Midrash tells us that when Moses gathered the people as a community to share with them these two national initiatives – the Sanctuary and Shabbat – his message to all future generations was that on Shabbat they should gather as communities to learn and be inspired together.[3]

Both of these community-forging enterprises – building the Sanctuary and keeping Shabbat – bring the Divine presence into the world[4] and generate immense spiritual energy, because God's presence is felt more intensely within a community. That is why communal prayer with a *minyan* is more powerful spiritually.[5] Similarly, learning Torah is considered a more sanctified and Godly experience in a communal setting.[6]

A similar concept applies to mitzvahs in general – as the verse says: "In the multitudes of the people is the glory of the King."[7] Public gatherings to promote or perform a mitzvah are vital for developing a sense of shared purpose – a shared vision and set of values. We strengthen and inspire each other when we gather together as a community.

Being a Jew is deeply connected to the idea of community. As a child first learns to speak, we teach them this verse about community:[8] "The Torah was commanded to us through Moses; it is the heritage of the community of Jacob."[9]

Community is deeply connected to our collaborating to fulfill the mitzvahs. There is no one Jew who can fulfill all 613 commandments. Some commandments apply only to Kohanim and others only to Levi'im. Some apply only to men and others only to women. Some apply only to kings and others only to judges. Some apply only to agriculture or to the legal system, and others only to commerce or the military.

And yet, somehow, *all* of the mitzvahs apply to *all* Jews. How is this possible? The answer is that keeping the mitzvahs – and being Jewish – is a communal, collaborative project.[10] "All of Israel is responsible as guarantors for one another."[11] We are all partners, unified by our common purpose and shared responsibility.

We feel this most intensely on Shabbat – the day when we leave our often-siloed existence and meld into a community. Its rhythms have united Jewish life around the world and across the ages; on Shabbat, we all read the same Torah portion, light the same candles, recite the same Kiddush, refrain from the same acts of work, enjoy the same festivities, say the same prayers, sit together around the table as a family for three meals. On Shabbat, we become one nation, keeping the same Shabbat, creating a horizontal community of Jews across continents and a vertical community of Jews across history.

Building community also means treating one another with respect and kindness. It means avoiding the fragmentation caused by gossip, insult, and conflict. Disunity – a breakdown in community – undermines the entire enterprise of the Torah, which is about creating spiritual community.[12]

We see this from the statement in the Talmud that the only "vessel" that can contain blessing is peace.[13] The "blessing" referred to is the Torah, which can only exist in this world when the Jewish People are unified.[14] The Torah describes how "Israel encamped by the mountain"[15] prior to the giving of the Torah. The verb "encamped" refers to the entire nation, but is written in the singular form – the message here is that the entire Jewish People were united for the purpose of receiving the Torah "like one person with one heart."[16]

Shabbat is the day we come together with "one heart" – the day we build community.

Chapter Notes

1 Exodus 35:1

2 Exodus 39:32

3 Midrash, Yalkut Shimoni on Torah 408

4 Sfat Emet, Exodus, Vayakhel 5636, on Exodus 35:1-2

5 Talmud, Berachot 8a; Rambam, Mishne Torah, Hilchot Tefilla 8:1; Shulchan Aruch, O.C. 90:9; Mishna Berura 90:28

6 Pirkei Avot 3:7; see Talmud, Megilla 3b

7 Proverbs 14:28

8 Talmud, Sukka 42a; Rambam, Mishne Torah, Hilchot Talmud Torah 1:6; Shulchan Aruch, Y.D. 245:5

9 Deuteronomy 33:4

10 Ohr HaChaim, Exodus 39:32; Meshech Chochmah, Exodus 19:8

11 Talmud, Sanhedrin 27b; Talmud, Shevuot 39a; Midrash, Bamidbar Rabba 10:5; Midrash, Sifra, Bechukotai 7:5, based on Leviticus 26:37; Midrash, Tanchuma, Nitzavim 2:1. This philosophical concept carries halachic ramifications, see Talmud, Rosh Hashana 29a with Rashi; Rambam, Mishne Torah, Hilchot Berachot 1:10; Shulchan Aruch, O.C. 167:19, 213:2, 273:4.

12 See Chapter 9 above.

13 Mishna, Uktzin 3:12; see Jerusalem Talmud, Berachot 2:4.

14 Ohel Yaakov, Nasso, s.v. *od nuchal*, based on Deuteronomy 11:26

15 Exodus 19:2

16 Rashi, Exodus 19:2, citing Midrash, Mechilta D'Rabbi Yishmael 19:2

HAPPINESS

32 | Happiness

The "day of your happiness"[1] is how the Torah describes Shabbat. We have seen how the day enables us to create ourselves through character and perspectives. In this part, we explore the ways in which Shabbat guides us to find happiness.[2]

The Talmud describes Shabbat as a gift, given to us by God from among His most precious treasures.[3] Like any gift, it is a sign of the love and kindness of the Giver and His wish to brighten our lives and make us happy.

By informing what we do and what we don't do on Shabbat, the *halacha* gives us a Divine recipe for a "day of happiness" – and, by extension, the wisdom we need to find joy in everything we do, all the time.

Shabbat teaches us a number of life lessons and skills for finding happiness:

1. We don't wait for it – we live proactively in ways that open us to happiness. Keeping Shabbat, which requires effort and intentionality, teaches us that real happiness does not come without conscious effort. Happiness is not something external or elusive that we pursue – it's a state of being that emerges naturally from how we live. If it comes to us from external circumstances beyond our control, it will always be transitory, passing when the novelty

wears off or circumstances change. But when we learn the life skills to access happiness, it becomes part of who we are.

2. Character sets the stage for happiness. When we work on becoming humble, generous, idealistic, wise, trusting, growing, optimistic people, we find true inner happiness. A selfish, arrogant person will struggle to be happy. A short-sighted, small-minded person is never happy for long. Lasting happiness is built on good character. And Shabbat gives us the tools to develop it.

3. Meaning and purpose are essential elements of happiness. The perspectives Shabbat provides illuminate our lives with purpose. Knowing that we have a Creator. That He is close and cares about us. That our lives have meaning. That our mission is broad. That we are God's partners in creation. That there is a World to Come. All of these foundational perspectives pave the way to deep and enduring happiness.

In the following eight chapters, we explore eight other lessons and life skills for happiness that Shabbat teaches us.

[1] Numbers 10:10 as per Midrash, Sifrei, Bamidbar 77. See Likutei Sichot Vol. 33, Beha'alotcha 2, which refers to the Sifrei and explains the differences – halachic and philosophical – between the concept of happiness on Shabbat and Yom Tov.

[2] The idea that forms the basis for this part of the book, that Shabbat is perfectly designed by God to be a day of enjoyment and happiness, is based on Rabbi Yerucham Levovitz, Daat Torah, Bamidbar, Parshat Beha'alotcha, p. 84-86. He refers to Shabbat as his main case study to support his view that the mitzvahs were designed to be the best way for us to live in terms of maximizing happiness in this world. See above, Chapter 2, for more on this idea. He supports his approach by referring to the Ibn Ezra and Ramban in their commentaries to Leviticus 18:5. See also Shelah, Torah SheBichtav, Mishpatim, Derech Chaim 4.

[3] Talmud, Shabbat 10b

33 | Free Yourself

When we are overburdened, our time and mind space for happiness is constrained. To open ourselves to happiness, we need to feel free.

At the time the Jewish People were slaves in Egypt, Pharaoh recognized this. When Moses said, "Let my people go,"[1] Pharaoh's reaction was to intensify their labor: "Let the people's work be made more difficult."[2] Pharaoh did not want a rebellion on his hands, so he tried to crush the spirit of the Jews by making them work harder. He believed that if he kept them busy, they would be too exhausted and distracted to indulge their hopes for freedom.

The Midrash tells us that Pharaoh actually removed their right to rest on Shabbat.[3] Previously, Moses had managed to negotiate Shabbat as a day off for the Jewish People,[4] which gave them time and space to restore themselves – physically, emotionally, and spiritually – and to find hope for the future. Shabbat was their island of freedom. To dash their hopes, Pharaoh took away their Shabbat respite and made them work every day of the week.

When we keep Shabbat, we remember that freedom is such a fundamental and precious gift. We remind ourselves of, and give thanks for, the kindness that God did for us in liberating us from slavery, granting us the gift of freedom for all time:[5] "Keep the Shabbat day to make it holy... and remember that you were slaves in Egypt and the Lord your God took you out from there."[6]

We are able to enjoy freedom today because God liberated us from slavery generations ago[7] – and yet, the quest for freedom remains.

There are other forms of slavery still prevalent today. During the week, we are assailed by the heavy burdens of our work and by all the stresses and pressures of the daily administration of our lives. Shabbat is about liberating ourselves from these taskmasters. On Shabbat, we unburden ourselves from everything we carry during the week. When we cast off our work burdens, we have the headspace to enjoy the day. Without this freedom, the load of responsibilities we carry can overshadow all our experiences and block the path to happiness.

This freedom is not just the physical respite from work. It is the mental freedom of knowing there is not even the possibility of doing it. The verse says: "Six days you shall labor and accomplish all your work, and the seventh day is Shabbat."[8] But how do you "accomplish all your work?" Is it even possible to complete everything you have to do in just six days? The Midrash explains this verse to mean that when Shabbat arrives, we should feel *as if* we have finished all our work.[9]

In fact, we never can get it all done. But on Shabbat, we can let go of the burden, because we have to stop. It is that one day in the week when we can feel completely calm because there is no pressure to work and carry out our regular daily tasks – simply because we are not allowed to. During the week, even when we take a break, the burden of our work still hangs over us. But on Shabbat, our mental load is lifted. At God's instruction, we put everything aside without any guilt. We feel the calm and peace of mind that comes with knowing we can slow down and relax because our work is done. We are truly free.

The quest for freedom goes deeper. It is also spiritual. When we are consumed with keeping up with the unrelenting demands of our lives, we can become distracted from our priorities, becoming slaves to ambition and materialism.[10] We remove these self-imposed shackles by setting aside a day when everything stops – when we are relieved of our spiritual enslavement and free to reconnect with our higher purpose.

This insight also emerges from our experience of slavery in Egypt, during which time Moses – understanding that freedom is more than physical respite – composed special Shabbat readings, which were later included in the Book of Psalms,[11] to give the Jewish People the faith and inspiration they needed to face their ongoing oppression at the hands of Pharaoh.[12]

Shabbat offers us the same sanctuary today that it did to our ancestors in Egypt – freedom to rise above the daily struggles of life. It is a day when our burdens are lifted. No matter what we are going through, whether physical hardship, emotional upheaval or spiritual malaise, we have Shabbat to bring us respite and reorient our lives. It enables us to breathe again and to focus on what is truly important.

And this freedom that Shabbat provides belongs to us all, equally.[13] When Shabbat arrives, every Jew – rich and poor, man, woman and child – is freed from the burdens of work to enjoy the day in dignity and tranquility. Regardless of one's circumstances, freedom, dignity, joy, and comfort fill Jewish homes the moment Shabbat begins. It does not matter what burdens we carry or what status we command – on Friday afternoon, as the sun sets, we are invited to leave our worries behind and experience real freedom, together, as equals.

And when we do that, we open ourselves to happiness.

Chapter Notes

1. Exodus 5:1

2. Exodus 5:9

3. Midrash, Shemot Rabba 5:18

4. Midrash, Shemot Rabba 1:28

5. Rambam, Guide for the Perplexed 2:31

6. Deuteronomy 5:12-15

7. Pesach Haggada

8. Exodus 20:9-10

9. Midrash, Mechilta D'Rabbi Yishmael 20:9, cited by Rashi on Exodus 20:9

10. See Rabbi Moshe Chaim Luzzatto, Mesilat Yesharim, Ch. 2, who links Pharaoh's enslavement with the spiritual enslavement caused by distraction and demands of life.

11. See Chapter 11 above, note 16, and Chapter 13 above, note 8.

12. Emet LeYaakov, Exodus 5:9, based on Talmud, Bava Batra 14b. See Chapter 11 above for more.

13. See Exodus 20:10; Deuteronomy 5:14.

34 | See What's in Front of You

A key ingredient of happiness is to live in the moment. To open our eyes to what lies right in front of us. To open our hearts to the wonders all around us.

During the rush of the week, the Talmud says that we lose part of our eyesight, which is then restored when we say Kiddush on Friday night, glancing at the Shabbat candles and the wine as we do so.[1] We learn from this that Shabbat enables us to see the world with new eyes – with perspective, clarity, and wisdom, which can be lost in the rush of our lives.[2]

Shabbat allows us to truly see our blessings. Suddenly, we can appreciate the deep flavor of the wine and the warm glow of the candles. When we rush around, living life at high speed, we miss out on so much. On Shabbat, we slow down, the frenzy ceases and our lives come into focus.

Shabbat teaches us to truly appreciate the wonder of our world; to savor the pleasures created for us with so much Divine love, to grasp the power and beauty of our most precious relationships, to feel the sublime gift of life itself. It is the day we are able to taste the sweetness of this world and celebrate it fully through the power of appreciation – the gateway to happiness.

On Shabbat, we set aside the natural human drive to acquire and allow ourselves the joy of appreciating what we have.[3] As Pirkei

Avot teaches, a truly wealthy person is someone "who takes joy in their portion."[4]

The Talmud[5] records a revealing conversation between the Roman Caesar[6] and Rabbi Yehoshua. The Caesar asked the Rabbi, "Why does your food smell so good on Shabbat?" to which the sage replied: "There is a very special spice we put into the food, called Shabbat." The Caesar then asked him if he could have some of this special ingredient, and Rabbi Yehoshua answered that only one who keeps Shabbat can enjoy its unique flavor. To really experience the world to its fullest, we must taste Shabbat.

The laws of Shabbat force us to slow down because we can't do the things that distract and pressure us. The pace of the day enables us to enjoy this world. We can take our gifts for granted. But once a week, we pause, breathe deeply and savor life's blessings. It is a day of giving thanks to God for creating such a beautiful world, for giving us a life full of blessings. It is a day of enjoying and appreciating life's simple pleasures – being with loved ones, discovering Divine wisdom, savoring delicious food, sleeping or taking a walk. By slowing down, we appreciate everything on a much deeper level.

When God finished creating the world, He looked at "everything He had created, and behold it was very good."[7] He set aside Shabbat as the day to invite His friends – all of us – to celebrate and cherish the home He created for us to live in.[8] Shabbat reminds us that God created our world and calls on us to celebrate and appreciate the magnificence of His artistry – the beauty of nature, the majesty of the human spirit, the awesome brilliance of every aspect of His creation. And to savor all these blessings.

The Talmud[9] lists three things that dim our eyes if we do not perceive them properly: the rainbow, the leader of the Sanhedrin, and the priests when they bless the people. When we see these three things, we should be able to feel, even *perceive*, the presence of God, and if not – if we aren't looking at them properly – it means our vision and perspective is impaired.

In a rainbow, we can see the magnificence of the physical world; God's awesome creativity and the beauty and perfection with which He created our world. When we see the leader of the Sanhedrin, a great Torah scholar, we are inspired by the greatness of mind, the purity of soul and refinement of character a person can achieve with the God-given potential within.

And when the priests bless the people, we feel the presence of God in the power of human love and compassion. Priests are called to "bless Your people with love,"[10] and to open their hands[11] as they do so as a symbol of love and generosity of spirit. When we experience the beauty of human love – when we see the potency and purity of the love between a mother and her baby, or feel closeness to another person – we feel the presence of God, the One Who created the human capacity for love.

We are creatures of habit, which can dull our sense of inspiration, or "dim our eyes," preventing us from noticing the constant miracles that surround us. Seeing these miracles is to live with a constant sense of wonder, which enables us to be happy.

The Talmud says that rain is a greater miracle than the revival of the dead.[12] When it rains after a drought, we thank God "for every drop that You brought down for us"[13] – we recognize that each drop is a God-given miracle.

We even thank God every day for constantly holding back the oceans from washing over the continents: "...Who spreads the land over the waters."[14] We can grasp this constant miracle by reflecting on another, more obvious, miracle described in the Torah. In the immediate aftermath of the Exodus, when the

Egyptian army pursued the Jewish People to the edge of the Sea of Reeds, the sea split to make a path of escape. God instructed Moses to stretch out his staff to initiate the miracle.[15] Then, once the Jews had safely reached the other side, again God told Moses to stretch out his staff and the sea returned to its former position.[16] Why did Moses have to stretch out his staff again, as if to perform another miracle? Surely all he had to do was withdraw the first miracle and the sea would return to its default position? The answer is that both actions – displacing and replacing the sea – are equally miraculous. The fact that God constantly holds back the ocean in its place so we can walk on dry land is *always* miraculous.[17]

In our Shabbat morning prayers, we recognize the warmth of the sun shining on our faces as a personal gift from God, which He recreates and renews for each of us: "...Who opens daily the doors of the gateways of the east" – referring to the rising of the sun – "and Who opens the windows of the Heavens; He removes the sun from its place; and illuminates the entire world for all who dwell in it."

When we rush through life we can lose our spiritual eyesight. Shabbat slows us down so that we can look at the world with fresh eyes, acutely aware of the beauty around us, appreciating everything as a gift from God. Living with appreciation, savoring our blessings, feeling grateful for everything we have, opens us to a life of happiness.

1 Talmud, Berachot 43b; Talmud, Shabbat 113b. See Darchei Moshe, O.C. 271:8; Machatzit HaShekel, O.C. 271:23; Mishna Berura 271:48.

2 See Shem MiShmuel, 5675 Numbers 16:1.

3 See Rabbi Mordechai Gifter, Pirkei Torah, on Deuteronomy 26:11.

4 Pirkei Avot 4:1

5 Talmud, Shabbat 119a

6 This is likely to have been the Emperor Hadrian (ruled 117-138 CE).

7 Genesis 1:31

8 Rav Achai Gaon, She'iltot 1:1

9 Talmud, Chagiga 16a. The interpretation of this passage in the Talmud as it appears here and the ideas that flow from it in the next few paragraphs are based on the oral discourses of Rabbi Yosef Dov Soloveitchik as recorded in "On Repentance", p.150 et seq., compiled by Rabbi Pinchas HaKohen Peli.

10 Talmud, Sota 39a

11 Rambam, Mishne Torah, Hilchot Tefilla 14:3; Shulchan Aruch, O.C. 128:10

12 Talmud, Taanit 7a. See also Midrash, Devarim Rabba 7:6.

13 Talmud, Berachot 59b; Talmud, Taanit 6b

14 Talmud, Berachot 60b; Siddur, Morning Blessings

15 Exodus 14:16

16 Exodus 14:26

17 Pirkei Torah, Exodus 14:26

35 | Find Holiness in Pleasure

The human drive for pleasure runs deep, but its relationship with happiness is complicated. A key insight into this relationship emerges from a profound comment made by one of our sages in a letter to his family.

Rabbi Eliyahu ben Shlomo Zalman, known as the Vilna Gaon, was embarking on the long and dangerous trip to the Land of Israel about 250 years ago, and he wrote a parting letter offering his family ethical guidance in his temporary absence.[1] At one point in the letter, he addresses the subject of pleasure, comparing the pleasures of the physical world to drinking salt water: the more you drink, the thirstier you become.

The reason we are not satiated by physical pleasure alone is that we are both body and soul, and we cannot ignore either one. If we nourish only the physical part of ourselves, we will feel empty and dissatisfied. Real satisfaction emerges only when the physical pleasures are connected to a higher purpose. When life is meaningful, when pleasure has a spiritual dimension, those same waters become refreshing, thirst-quenching.

The Midrash compares the relationship between the body and soul to the unlikely marriage of a peasant farmer and a princess.[2] The farmer tries to impress his new wife by bringing her his choicest crops, which do not mean anything to her with her royal upbringing. So, too, the things that the body derives so much pleasure from mean nothing to the soul – unless they are connected with meaning and purpose. When the physical world is used for a higher purpose, for doing good, it brings us deep satisfaction. When we view the gifts of the physical world through a spiritual lens, we feel connected to that higher purpose. On the other hand, because we have a spiritual essence, the pursuit of pleasure for its own sake will ultimately leave us dissatisfied – like drinking salt water.

Shabbat teaches us that for physical pleasure to bring happiness, it must be connected to meaning. When Isaiah the Prophet describes Shabbat as a day of pleasure, he refers to physical and spiritual pleasure: "And you shall call Shabbat pleasure... and take pleasure in God..."[3] It is the day we remind ourselves that God created our world and all its abundant blessings and pleasures.[4]

The day offers us a beautiful, balanced formula for connecting physical and spiritual pleasure, which is the secret to enjoying life and finding happiness. Shabbat shows us that holiness and pleasure are intertwined.[5] The sanctity of the day is expressed through the pleasures of the day.[6] In fact, the very call to sanctify the day ("Remember the Shabbat day to make it holy"[7]) is fulfilled by the pleasurable experience of drinking wine[8] after reciting the words of the Kiddush (literally, "sanctification"). And our "extra soul" on Shabbat gives us the capacity to enjoy the physical pleasures of the day more intensely.[9]

The holiness of Shabbat is expressed through the combination of physical and spiritual pleasure. It is a day of delicious food, fine clothing, refreshing naps – and also a day of prayer and Torah learning, of connecting to God.[10] It is a day for the pleasures of loving relationships, of being together with family and friends.[11]

In particular, it is a day for enjoying the physical and emotional pleasures of the sacred bond between husband and wife.[12] The marriage ceremony is called *kiddushin* – from the word *kedusha*, "holiness"[13] – precisely because it represents the ultimate connection between physical pleasure and the higher purpose of forging a loving relationship. Marriage ennobles husband and wife as individuals, enabling them to reach their full potential, and, as a couple, empowering them to fulfill the sacred mission of building the world through family.[14]

The physical pleasures of Shabbat enhance the sanctity of the day, which in turn uplift the physical experiences, creating a virtuous cycle – revealing the elusive connection between pleasure and happiness.

Chapter Notes

[1] The Vilna Gaon's letter, Iggeret HaGra, written to his family before embarking on a journey to the Land of Israel, has endured as a cherished text and continues to inspire and guide us. The Vilna Gaon's journey was aborted, but some of his students subsequently embarked upon their own journeys to the Holy Land, and set the groundwork for an impetus of emigration to Israel from Eastern Europe during the early 1800s.

[2] Midrash, Vayikra Rabba 4:2

[3] Isaiah 58:13-14

[4] Kad HaKemach, Shabbat

[5] The concept of Shabbat combining the physical and the spiritual presented in this chapter is based on the writings of Rabbi Natan Tzvi Finkel, Ohr HaTzafun, Vol. 2, Article 23, p.132-135. These ideas are connected to the ones articulated by Rabbi Yerucham Levovitz referred to above in Chapters 2 and 32. Rabbi Levovitz was mentored and taught by Rabbi Finkel, which makes the connection between their ideas significant.

[6] Talmud, Pesachim 68b

[7] Exodus 20:8

[8] Talmud, Pesachim 105b-106a; Rambam, Mishne Torah, Hilchot Shabbat 29:6-7; Shulchan Aruch, O.C. 271:3-4, 10

[9] Rashi on Talmud, Beitza 16a and on Talmud, Taanit 27b

[10] See Chapter 3 above and Chapter 7 above.

[11] See Chapter 30 above and Chapter 37 below.

[12] Talmud, Ketubot 62b; Talmud, Bava Kamma 82a; Rambam, Mishne Torah, Hilchot Deot 5:4, Hilchot Ishut 14:1; Shulchan Aruch, O.C. 240:1, 280:1, E.H 76:2

[13] See Taz, E.H. 34:2

[14] Genesis 1:28; Isaiah 45:18; Rambam, Sefer HaMitzvot, Positive Mitzvah 212, Mishne Torah, Hilchot Ishut, chapter 15; Sefer HaChinuch, mitzvah 1; Shulchan Aruch, E.H. chapter 1. See also Talmud, Yevamot 62b; Talmud, Sanhedrin 76b.

36 | Be Ready for Renewal

One of the obstacles to happiness is boredom with life itself. It is feeling stale and uninspired, that life is an endlessly repetitive cycle, one day indistinguishable from the next.

Shabbat is a day apart; a day identifiably different from any other, arresting the feelings of listlessness and indifference that may oppress us. Most importantly, it is a day of renewal – an opportunity to replenish ourselves and refresh our outlook.

The concept of renewal is far deeper than physical rest.

Shabbat is described as "an eternal sign that six days God made heaven and earth, and on the seventh day He rested and was refreshed" – *vayinafash*.[1] The Hebrew word *vayinafash* literally means "and He was refreshed."[2] But how can we speak about God being refreshed? Does the Creator of the universe get tired and worn down?[3]

Clearly, we need to re-examine our understanding of the word *vayinafash*. One approach[4] is that it comes from the Hebrew word *nefesh*, meaning "soul." On the first Shabbat of history, God infused all of creation with a soul. Before the seventh day of Creation, the world lacked an animating life force, a spiritual dimension. But on that first Shabbat, *vayinafash,* God gave a *nefesh* – a soul and spirit – to the world, thereby completing the work of the prior six days of Creation.

But this Divine infusion of soul and spiritual energy into the universe was not a once-off event. It happens every Shabbat. We learn this from the verse: "...six days God created heaven and earth."[5] There's a preposition missing. Grammatically, it should say, "*in* six days God created heaven and earth." One explanation[6] of this unusual phrasing is that God created the world to last *only* six days, whereafter it would automatically expire and disintegrate – were it not for Shabbat.

The universe exists in a recurring seven-day cycle. Every six days, the world comes to an end – at which point Shabbat arrives to renew and refresh it. Every Shabbat, God breathes new energy – new life – into the world. And into each of us, too. Shabbat refreshes us physically, emotionally, and spiritually, giving us a chance to breathe. Just as God animated Adam with "the breath of life,"[7] God gives us the revitalizing breath of Shabbat every week. The source of our energy and lifeforce is the Divine soul within us.[8] And every Shabbat, we access our soul in a new, deeper way. Shabbat has the power to revive our soul, rejuvenating us with a renewed spiritual energy that flows into every part of our being, enriching our relationships and uplifting our lives.

Shabbat inspires us to *live* with this mindset of renewal.[9] It guides us to see the world as new and fresh with possibility, which opens us to happiness and inspiration. It prevents us from stagnating and becoming bored with life. It teaches us that we are living in a world that at any one point is no more than six days old, and that every week is the chance to start afresh. It inspires in us an awareness and appreciation of the ongoing miracles of creation.

And it reminds us that God renews and refreshes His world constantly.[10] Seasons change, the time to harvest comes and goes, cells die and are replaced, babies begin to walk and then run. Each morning we wake up to a familiar world in a familiar body, but, in fact, everything – including our mind and our soul – is being renewed all the time. The universe and everything in it exist in a dynamic state of Divine "re-creation."

This idea is expressed through the present-tense wording of the blessings formulated by the sages of the Talmud.[11] Before eating a fruit, we say: "Blessed are You... Who creates the fruit of the tree."[12] We are not just thanking God for having created fruit trees at some point in the distant past, or for setting in motion the laws of nature that "automatically" produce fruit – we are thanking Him for constantly refreshing and recreating the world, and for creating *this* fruit that we enjoy *now*. This is why it is not enough to say this blessing once for a lifetime. Every time we partake of the earth's wondrous bounty, we acknowledge that God made it just for us.

Other blessings are also phrased in the present tense: "Who *brings forth* bread from the earth"; "Who *creates* the fruit of the vine."[13] In the morning when we wake up, we give thanks to the One: "Who *opens* the eyes of the blind"; "Who *straightens* the bent."[14] We also express in the present tense our gratitude to God for renewing our capacity to learn every day, and granting us insight into His wisdom: "Who *teaches* Torah to His people," and "Who *gives* the Torah."[15] With each blessing, we acknowledge our personal relationship with God, and thank Him for constantly renewing ourselves and our world each day.

Through Shabbat, we are guided to live in a seven-day cycle; to appreciate on a daily basis the newness and freshness of the world each week. God teaches us by example, by remaking and renewing the world constantly – challenging us to live with newness, to view the world from a fresh and inspired perspective. He re-creates the world and makes it new all the time; we, too, should strive to live our lives with newness and freshness, every single day.

Living with newness also means never slipping into complacency, which leads to boredom. The Talmud says that we face new kinds of temptation all the time.[16] What once seemed so enticing loses its appeal, and we must grapple with new challenges to our integrity and character. Life is dynamic and we should never be complacent about what we have achieved, nor think that our job is done. As Pirkei Avot says: "Do not be sure of yourself until the day of your death."[17]

Shabbat teaches us that there is no status quo; that the world we live in is constantly being renewed and recreated, which makes it an exciting place to live. It reminds us that we can recreate ourselves and our lives, that we must not allow ourselves to feel constrained by self-imposed limitations and by being mired in old ways of doing things.

Shabbat reminds us that the world we live in is dynamic and fluid. Our Divine liberation from slavery, with all its awesome miracles, to which Shabbat testifies, reminds us that laws of nature that seem fixed – slaves in Egypt were never freed[18] and seas don't split – can change. Just as the world changes, we, too, are capable of change, and must rise to the challenge of living our lives in an inspired way, constantly reinventing and refreshing ourselves.

Shabbat empowers us to feel truly alive – to see ourselves and our world as dynamic and fresh, alive with possibility, to be ready for renewal and excited with life.

1 Exodus 31:17

2 See Rashi, Exodus 31:17, based on Targum Onkelos.

3 See Isaiah 40:28.

4 Ohr HaChaim, Genesis 2:2. See also Rashi and Ibn Ezra on Exodus 31:17.

5 Exodus 31:17

6 Ohr HaChaim, Genesis 2:3, based on Exodus 20:11

7 Genesis 2:7

8 Derech Hashem 1:3:7

9 The ideas presented in the next few paragraphs are drawn from Rabbi Natan Tzvi Finkel, Ohr HaTzafun, Vol. 2, Article 18, p. 100-105.

10 Lamentations 3:23; Zohar 2:260b; Tomer Devora 1:1. We praise God for this constant cycle of recreation in the blessings before Shema of Shacharit.

11 Talmud, Berachot 35b

12 Talmud, Berachot 35a

13 Talmud, Berachot 35a

14 Talmud, Berachot 60b

15 Talmud, Berachot 11b

16 Talmud, Kiddushin 30b, based on Genesis 6:5 and Psalms 37:32-33

17 Pirkei Avot 2:5

18 Midrash, Mechilta D'Rabbi Yishmael 18:11; Rashi, Exodus 18:9

37 | **Nurture Your Relationships**

Thriving, loving relationships are a vital ingredient for happiness. We have three essential relationships: with God, with the people in our lives, and with ourselves.[1] These relationships are the core of our identity and, when we nurture them, the source of our deepest happiness.

They are also the heart of the Torah's holistic system for creating a "world of loving friendship."[2] This phrase distills the Torah to its essence – the commandments are the pathways to forming and nurturing loving relationships with other people, with God, and with ourselves.

Shabbat encapsulates this vision: it is described by the Talmud as an emblem, "a sign," of the Torah system as a whole.[3] On Shabbat, we nurture these three core relationships in our lives, infusing them with love and meaning. One of the songs we sing on Shabbat reflects this, invoking the day as a "beloved friend."[4] Shabbat is the day to rediscover and reconnect with all our "beloved friends" – with God, with the people in our lives and with ourselves. We welcome in Shabbat with the words of *Lecha Dodi*[5] – "Come, my friend," which can refer to God or to the people around us. We are all friends on Shabbat.

Relationships need our time and focus. We need to be present and give them real attention and emotional energy. When we do, we find happiness. Shabbat gives us the time and meaningful moments to nurture our relationships.

We take a break from the rough and tumble of life to be with the people who are most important to us, giving full, undivided attention to those we love, pouring our hearts into our precious family relationships in particular.[6]

It is also a day for reconnecting with God, which we do through reaffirming our faith in Him as the Creator of the universe, and through prayer and learning Torah. Shabbat reframes our relationship with God, enabling us to view the Torah's commandments as guidance and instruction from a loving, nurturing Parent. And just as we devote ourselves to those we love – we keep the mitzvahs out of love for God.[7]

We connect with God during the week through His commandments, which are designed to nurture this bond. Take prayer, for example.[8] Just as a devoted husband and wife find time to speak with each other in the middle of a busy day, we deepen our relationship with God when we pray three times a day.[9] Prayer, however, is only a relatively short part of a typical day – on Shabbat, we have an *entire* day to nurture our awareness of God's presence and our spiritual connection to Him.[10]

Shabbat also helps us reconnect with ourselves. It gives us the time and space to be alone with our thoughts and feelings, without distraction – to rediscover our inner voice and our authentic selves, which is so vital to finding happiness. To know who we are and what we want from life requires quiet time to listen to ourselves think and feel.

With its spiritual experiences, Shabbat offers us the opportunity to reconnect with our soul, the essence of who we are. When we give in to negative behavior, we become alienated from ourselves. Our conscience alerts us with feelings of guilt and disconnectedness. This is why the Hebrew word for idolatry is *avoda zara,* literally, "foreign worship" – because it alienates us from God, but also, significantly, from ourselves. "There shall not be a strange god within you"[11] refers to idolatry, but also, says the Talmud,[12] to moments when we lose control of ourselves. Losing our temper, for example, is like worshiping a strange god, estranging us from our pure, Godly essence.

Any lack of connectedness – to God, to other people, to ourselves – means a dislocation from the world of loving friendship. Consider the connection between the Hebrew words *zar* (foreign or estranged) and *achzar* (cruel).[13] Being cruel to another person is an expression of (and caused by) our estrangement from them.[14] Significantly, the Talmud characterizes refusing to forgive someone who has wronged us – after they show remorse by apologizing with sincerity and repairing any damage caused – an act of cruelty.[15] It is an expression of complete estrangement from the other person. Alienation from God and His call to us to live a life of giving and goodness is a form of self-cruelty.[16]

When we become estranged from God, from people or from ourselves, it leads to feelings of dislocation and isolation, feelings that make happiness impossible. When we nurture our most precious relationships – when we enter a "world of loving friendship" – we feel connection and love. We feel happy.

Chapter Notes

¹ Pirkei Avot 1:2 with the commentaries of Maharal, Tiferet Yisrael, Rabbi S.R. Hirsch, and Sfat Emet

² The ideas in this chapter are based on the writings of Rabbi Shlomo Wolbe in his work "Sefer Olam HaYedidut," based on the talks he gave at kibbutzim and towns across Israel in response to the spiritual awakening in Israeli society after the Six Day War.

³ Talmud, Menachot 36b, based on Exodus 31:16. In fact, Shabbat is equivalent to all other mitzvahs combined, see Jerusalem Talmud, Berachot 1:5, based on Nechemiah 9:14; Jerusalem Talmud, Nedarim 3:9, based on Exodus 16:28-29, Ezekiel 20:13, and Nechemiah 9:13-14; Midrash, Shemot Rabba 25:12; Midrash, Devarim Rabba 4:4; Rambam, Mishne Torah, Hilchot Shabbat 30:15; Ramban, Genesis 27:7, Exodus 20:8, Leviticus 19:30.

⁴ Mah Yedidut. This song is an acrostic where the first letter of each stanza spells the name "Menachem," which suggests that it was composed either by Rabbi Menachem ben Helbo Kara (1015-1085) or Rabbi Menachem of Le Mans in the 900s.

⁵ Lecha Dodi was composed by Rabbi Shlomo HaLevi Alkabetz (1500-1576) in Tzfat, Israel, then a small town that saw a surge in Torah scholarship and life during the 1500s. Lecha Dodi was warmly embraced throughout the Jewish world and was subsequently incorporated into the Siddur as a centerpiece of the Kabbalat Shabbat service.

⁶ See Chapter 30 above.

⁷ Pirkei Avot 1:3

⁸ Prayer is an intimate conversation with God. See Talmud, Berachot 31a; Talmud, Sanhedrin 22a; Shulchan Aruch, O.C. 98:1

⁹ Talmud, Berachot 26b; Rambam, Mishne Torah, Hilchot Tefilla 1:5-9; Shulchan Aruch, O.C. 89:1, 233:1, 237:1

¹⁰ Talmud, Pesachim 68b

¹¹ Psalms 81:10

¹² Talmud, Shabbat 105b

¹³ Rabbi S.R. Hirsch, Deuteronomy 32:33

¹⁴ Rambam, Mishne Torah, Hilchot Aveil 13:12

[15] Talmud, Bava Kama 92a; Rambam, Mishne Torah, Hilchot Teshuva 2:9-10; Shulchan Aruch, O.C. 606:1, C.M. 422:1

[16] Rambam, Mishne Torah, Hilchot Taaniyot 1:3

38 | Rest Actively

We won't find happiness in a life of only recreation and leisure, free from demands, challenges, and obligations. To create real, lasting happiness, we need to work, struggle, and contribute. We need to live an active, productive life. This idea goes to the heart of Shabbat.[1]

The Midrash[2] recounts how, after God finished creating the world, He noted that one thing was missing – *menucha,* superficially translated as "rest." So He created Shabbat. Shabbat didn't just materialize when God stopped creating on the seventh day – Shabbat was, itself, a Divine creation like everything else in the universe.[3] The Midrash compares this to a king who has prepared a magnificent hall and wedding canopy, but is still waiting for the bride. So, too, when God created the world, the whole of creation awaited the bride – Shabbat – which we refer to when we sing the words of the beautifully poetic prayer *Lecha Dodi,*[4] welcoming in Shabbat as a bride.

This analogy to a bride overturns a possible misconception of Shabbat. If it is simply a day of rest, an absence of stress and demands, rather than the presence of something positive, why is it symbolized by a bride? A bride is very much a presence at a wedding; she is the beauty, the meaning, the purpose of the event.

It emerges that *menucha*, rather than simply "rest," is something active, positive, and creative – a real presence, like a bride at a wedding, filling the world with the beauty of purpose. Shabbat is not simply a day of rest, it is a day of action, filled with rich experiences and meaningful activity – spending time with family, enjoying festive meals together and singing, sharing Torah ideas, praying, connecting with a community, connecting with God. Shabbat shows us that happiness – deep contentment and tranquility of spirit – comes from living actively and purposefully, from doing good and living in harmony with our deepest inner nature – with our soul, which was not created to be inactive.

God created us to be active, productive. An analogy is given of a river flowing down towards the ocean. When something obstructs its course, the river becomes turbulent with rapids and currents. God created each of us with a soul, and the purpose to do good in this world, to fulfill His commandments and carry sacred responsibilities. In the same way that a river naturally flows down, toward the ocean, our souls naturally 'flow' up, toward God. All things yearn to return to their source. When we interrupt that natural flow, the result is tension and turbulence. Fulfillment and inner peace come only from acting in harmony with God's will, from doing good and living with purpose. When we strive simply to avoid duty and obligation, when we cast off our responsibility to contribute positively to the world, when we seek only purposeless leisure, we don't find peace of mind or happiness. On the contrary, we become restless and uneasy, losing our equilibrium.

The Siddur[5] describes Shabbat as offering us "rest of love and generosity, rest of truth and faith." The emotional and physical effort needed to nurture true love is considerable, but inner peace and deep contentment emerge from investing our energy in our most precious relationships. Shabbat also helps us become generous people and true givers – a way of living that requires real effort. Truth and faith likewise do not come easily. The study of Torah is all about the pursuit of truth, and requires substantial mental and emotional effort.[6] Faith in God requires intellectual, emotional, and spiritual work as it develops and deepens over a lifetime.[7] And yet all this real effort brings with it the rewards of Shabbat – "rest filled with peace and tranquility, calm and security."[8] The message is simple: when we live actively and productively, fulfilling our higher purpose, we find peace – and create happiness.

Shabbat is a day of growth and upward striving, which brings inner peace. The Talmud says that when we part from someone, we say, "go *to* peace" rather than "go *in* peace."[9] The search for peace is a journey in which we are constantly changing, creating and growing. Inner peace is not a destination. It is not an undisturbed state of inactivity. Shabbat teaches us that we will find peace when we journey *toward* it; when we devote ourselves to becoming happier, more fulfilled people.

Going back to the dawn of creation, when God said that the world was empty without its bride – without Shabbat – we now have a glimpse of an understanding of what He meant. Without Shabbat and what it represents, the world is an empty, physical shell – strikingly beautiful and brilliant, but without soul, without meaning and purpose – like a wedding hall, decorated and magnificent, but without its bride.

The lesson for us is clear: happiness does not come from seeking a life empty of challenge and contribution – it comes from living actively, from learning and growing, from doing good deeds and contributing, from living with Divine purpose.

Chapter Notes

[1] The ideas in this chapter are based on the writings of Rabbi Elya Meir Bloch, Shiurei Daat, Shiur 17, Menuchat HaNefesh, p.109-116.

[2] Midrash, Bereishit Rabba 10:9

[3] See Genesis 2:2 with Rashi, based on Midrash, Bereishit Rabba 10:9.

[4] See Chapter 37 above, note 5.

[5] Shabbat Mincha Amidah

[6] Talmud, Berachot 63b; Talmud, Shabbat 83b; Talmud, Gittin 57b

[7] See Sefer HaChinuch, mitzvah 25.

[8] Shabbat Mincha Amidah

[9] Talmud, Berachot 64a

39 | **Find Your Ark**

Human beings seek out the adventure of achievement, but also the comfort of stability. We strive to go out into the world and do things – and to feel centered. Real happiness seems to require us to fulfill both of these competing needs. Our need for stability is intensified in a constantly changing world that sometimes leaves us feeling dislocated – from ourselves, and our families and communities.

Being centered is the feeling of self-possession, the sense that our lives are coherent and purposeful, our identity strong and clear, our mindset balanced and stable. This state of being is a crucial element of happiness. And Shabbat enables it.

A beautiful Shabbat song[1] poignantly evokes the image of a dove in search of rest: "On it [Shabbat] the dove found rest;[2] there shall rest the exhausted ones." The song references the dove that Noah sent from the Ark to scout for dry land after the great flood.[3] The dove flew around but couldn't find anywhere to rest; eventually it returned, exhausted – on Shabbat – to the Ark, where it finally found rest.[4]

Like the dove, during the week we fly from place to place, task to task, with nowhere to stop and rest. But at the end of an exhausting week, we return to Shabbat and find physical, emotional, and spiritual sanctuary; a haven of calm, our ark in a sea of chaos.[5] Returning to Shabbat each week is finding solace and stability in a turbulent world; finding our center, and with it, coherence and balance – all necessary ingredients for happiness.

Shabbat creates a rhythm for the week. Unlike the festivals that occur once a year, Shabbat is never more than six days away. We fly out into the world and return to our nest on Shabbat. We flit between shaping the world and retreating to consolidate our *inner* world. The dynamic is of going out and returning, extending and regrouping, expending and replenishing.

The song refers to "the exhausted ones." The ceaseless demands of the week exhaust us physically, but also emotionally and spiritually. We arrive at the doorstep of Shabbat drained of all our reserves. But over the course of 25 hours, we replenish those reserves. And we find stability and love. We retreat into the emotional warmth and safety of the Shabbat ark and reconnect with our loved ones in an atmosphere of peace and tranquility. After we have flitted from place to place, from one endeavor to the next, we return to source, like birds to our nest. We come home to Shabbat. We feel centered. We feel happy.

Shabbat is where we feel truly at home in the world. It is, more than anything, our spiritual home. Noah's Ark, too, was not only a place of physical safety – it was a haven of Divine values and spiritual sustenance in a world disconnected from ethics and kindness. The Torah describes the society of that time as a "world filled with lawlessness."[6] But Noah was "a righteous man, pure… who walked with God."[7] And the Ark he built was to be not only a physical refuge from the floodwaters, but a spiritual refuge from the corruption of the world. In a world submerged, Noah's Ark was a haven of life and light.

It was, most of all, a haven of kindness. Noah and his family spent all their time on the Ark caring for the animals within.[8] The sheer scale of feeding and cleaning and caring is difficult to imagine. And there weren't many people to share the load.

We can now begin to understand why God chose to save the world specifically through Noah's Ark. The generation of the flood was one characterized by the opposite of kindness. It was a society in which lawlessness and theft and cruelty were rampant. Hence, the process of restoring human civilization – of getting the project of Creation back on track – had to begin with building a world of loving-kindness.

God wanted the remnants of civilization to retreat into the sanctity of the Ark so that a new and improved society could emerge from the devastation.[9] The Hebrew word for flood comes from the root of the word for confusion and chaos.[10] The flood reflected a world turned upside down – dislocated, incoherent, in disarray. The world had lost its moral center. The Ark was the beginning of the process of reestablishing it.

That is why even when the floodwaters had dissipated, Noah had to wait for God's instruction before leaving the Ark.[11] He needed guidance on when the spiritual and moral work of the Ark was complete, and at what point his family could emerge to build a new world on the foundations of the Divine values of kindness and respect.

Like Noah's Ark, Shabbat is a place where coherence and balance are restored, a place of Divine clarity in an otherwise spiritually confusing and morally chaotic world.[12] Shabbat gives us a warm center around which to build our lives. It is the day we find our center, our ark – and with it, our happiness.

Chapter Notes

1. "Yom Shabbaton", a song traditionally sung at Shabbat lunch. The chorus begins *yona matza bo mano'ach*, "on it [Shabbat] the dove found rest". The song forms an acrostic that spells out the name of the author, "Yehuda," likely the liturgical poet Rabbi Yehuda HaLevi (1075-1141). In this interpretation of the song, the dove finds rest in Noah's Ark, which symbolizes Shabbat (see below note 5).

2. See Tikkunei Zohar 22b.

3. Genesis 8:8

4. Genesis 8:9; Tikkunei Zohar 22b

5. The notion of Shabbat being a haven from the chaotic week symbolized by Noah's Ark is addressed by Rabbi Sholom Noach Berezovsky, the Slonimer Rebbe, Netivot Shalom, Parshat Noach, p. 51 et seq.

6. Genesis 6:13

7. Genesis 6:9

8. Talmud, Sanhedrin 108b; Midrash, Tanchuma, Noach 9

9. This interpretation of the function of the Ark is offered by Rabbi Mordechai Gifter, Pirkei Torah, Genesis 8:15.

10. See Rashi, Genesis 6:17.

11. Genesis 8:15-17; Midrash, Kohelet Rabba 10:4; Pirkei Torah, Genesis 8:16

12. Netivot Shalom, Parshat Noach, p. 51 et seq., based on Tikkunei Zohar 140a.

40 | Make Your Life Whole

We are composed of conflicting forces – physical and spiritual, emotional and intellectual, altruistic and self-regarding; and multiple identities – individual, family, social, national, and universal. Because of this, we can feel scattered and fragmented, feelings that are incompatible with happiness. For our emotional well-being, we need to integrate and harmonize all these different dimensions of ourselves. Shabbat teaches us how to become whole.

Shabbat brings together the multifaceted dimensions of our lives. It is a day of personal development, and also of focus on family and community. It is a day with spiritual, intellectual, emotional, and physical aspects. Shabbat is an immersive experience that caters to every part of who we are. It shows us how we can harmonize all the different facets of our identity. It is this integration of physical and spiritual that brings harmony and wholeness. If either dimension is negated, we feel incomplete. True happiness comes from embracing all aspects of ourselves and becoming whole.

Shabbat offers a complete experience, satisfying every dimension of our being. Shabbat gives our lives coherence through a single, unifying moral vision and a sense of purpose.[1] It is a day we remind ourselves that all of creation has One Creator, Who unifies all of existence, and that He created the world using one master blueprint – the Torah.

HAPPINESS

The Torah itself is called a "song"[2] because music involves the distilling of disparate, often conflicting notes into one harmonious whole. The Talmud says that if the Jewish People did not accept the Torah, giving it a home and application in this world, then all of existence would have been engulfed by the primeval forces of chaos from the first day of Creation.[3] It is significant, therefore, that the Torah was given on Shabbat,[4] the day that reconnects us to its harmonizing vision for our lives. When we are whole, when all parts of our lives are unified in the service of a higher purpose, we feel at peace.

This integration goes to the heart of the Torah system, with mitzvahs that are custom-designed by our Creator for physical beings with a spiritual essence living in a physical world. It provides a plan to elevate the physical world by making it holy.[5]

This emerges in a dramatic debate between Moses and the angels at the moment God is about to give the Torah to the Jewish People. The Talmud[6] records that the angels object on the grounds that the Torah is too spiritual, perfect and precious to be given to fallible, mortal human beings. Moses responds by demonstrating that the Divine commandments are *only* relevant to human beings; that none of the Ten Commandments[7] – keeping Shabbat, honoring parents, the prohibitions against murdering, stealing or committing adultery, and all the others – apply to angels.

The Torah was not designed for angels, who lack all connection to the physical world. It was designed for complex human beings, as a song that brings harmony to our multifaceted existence.

"Shalom" comes from the root *shalem*, which means "complete."[8] Ultimate peace – and with it, true happiness – emerges from the harmony of all the elements of our lives and of existence in one, complete picture, reflected in the expression that captures it all:

"Shabbat shalom."[9] When we make music from the different, disparate notes of our lives, we feel whole and happy.

Chapter Notes

[1] See the chapters in Part 2: Perspectives.

[2] Deuteronomy 31:19

[3] Talmud, Shabbat 88a

[4] Talmud, Shabbat 86b

[5] Derech Hashem 1:1:4

[6] Talmud, Shabbat 88b-89a

[7] Exodus 20:1-14; Deuteronomy 5:6-18

[8] Maharal, Netivot Olam, Netiv HaShalom 1:7

[9] 'Shabbat shalom' is the standard Shabbat greeting, and the commentators offer various nuances in interpretation of this. See Shelah, Aseret HaDibrot, Shabbat, Ner Mitzvah 133; Ohr HaChaim, Leviticus 19:3; Ben Ish Chai, introduction to Parshat Naso.

IMPACT

41 | Impact

Shabbat is a force. It has the spiritual power of all our mitzvahs combined.[1] We have explored how it empowers us to create ourselves through building character, shaping perspectives and finding happiness.

But its potential impact is wider. It has the power to transform us not only as individuals and families, but as communities and even as a nation. It has the power to change the world.

In the next four chapters, we track the widening ripples of the impact of Shabbat – beginning with the essential 25-hour experience, to being the epicenter of our week, the soulmate of the Jewish People, and the bold idea we need to rise to the historic challenges and opportunities of our times.

Chapter Notes

[1] Jerusalem Talmud, Berachot 1:5, based on Nechemiah 9:14; Jerusalem Talmud, Nedarim 3:9, based on Exodus 16:28-29, Ezekiel 20:13, Nechemiah 9:13-14; Midrash, Shemot Rabba 25:12; Midrash, Devarim Rabba 4:4; Rambam, Mishne Torah, Hilchot Shabbat 30:15, based on Exodus 31:13, 17; Ramban on Genesis 27:7, Exodus 20:8, Leviticus 19:30.

42 | Our 25-Hour Home

The degree to which Shabbat impacts our character, perspectives and happiness depends on how completely immersive our 25-hour experience is. The more porous and fragmented we allow this time to be, the less impact it will have.

A way to understand the idea is to think about the physical spaces we inhabit. We designate a space for ourselves, constructing walls and a roof that serve the functional need of protecting us from the physical elements of the world. But then we infuse that space with love and care, with emotional warmth that transforms the lifeless structure from a house into a home, from something purely utilitarian into something nurturing and human. A sanctuary enriched by the people who occupy it.

Just as we do with our physical homes, Shabbat invites us to construct a home in time to hold us and the people in our lives.[1] Time is no less real than space. It permeates everything. It is inescapable. Together, space and time are the two critical framing elements of existence.[2] They define our lives. At its heart, Shabbat is a mitzvah of time, transforming it from a mechanical experience into something deeply personal and meaningful. Sunset on Friday means something completely different to any other sunset; we leave the week behind and enter Shabbat, a different dimension of time and existence.

IMPACT

Shabbat time has holiness independent of our subjective experience of it.³ God sanctified the seventh day at the beginning of Creation.⁴ He imbued Shabbat with a special spiritual energy that fills us and our world. We then partner with God by sanctifying Shabbat ourselves, reinforcing the holiness of the day.

By lighting candles and then later reciting Kiddush (literally, "sanctification") at the beginning of Shabbat, and reciting Havdalah at the end, we designate and dedicate the 25 hours of Shabbat that are both within time and transcend it, fulfilling our Divine mandate to sanctify Shabbat at the two moments it touches the days of the week.⁵

For the 25 hours between sunset on Friday and stars out on Saturday, we have the opportunity to transform a functional, impersonal unit of time into a sanctuary of peace, joy, togetherness, love, inspiration, spirituality, faith, and connection – to build a home in time, where we can transform our character and perspectives, and find happiness.

Just as a physical house needs solid walls and a roof to protect the people inside, our Shabbat home-in-time needs the protective walls and roof created by the *halacha*. These laws insulate us from all the daily distractions, burdens, and turbulence that afflict us during the week. They let us take shelter in the safety and tranquility of the 25 hours that become our new home and enable us to create ourselves and our family in a spirit of love and togetherness. Every breach of the *halacha* breaches the walls and roof of our Shabbat sanctuary, and impedes our ability to experience its true joy and power.

It is profound, therefore, that the laws of what we don't do on Shabbat are derived, as we have seen, from the 39 categories of creative work performed to construct the Sanctuary in the desert after the Jewish People left Egypt.⁶ The Sanctuary was a place where people would go to be inspired, educated, uplifted,

210

and transformed. The 39 acts of work created this sacred space – and, correspondingly, by refraining from them on Shabbat, we create a sanctuary in time[7] – 25 hours of sacred, uninterrupted time with God, family, and community, and with ourselves, enabling us to attain an entirely new elevated state of being.

As the sun sets on a Friday, we enter our 25-hour Shabbat home. Physically, the same place. Spiritually, completely new.

Chapter Notes

[1] See Rav Achai Gaon, She'iltot, 1:1.

[2] See Ramban on Genesis 1:5; Sforno on Genesis 1:1; Vilna Gaon, Aderet Eliyahu, on Genesis 1:1, that time is a creation of God like everything else in the universe.

[3] See Talmud, Berachot 49a; Rambam, Mishne Torah, Hilchot Tefilla 2:5, 2:11, Hilchot Seder HaTefillah 3:4, 3:7, 5:3, Hilchot Shabbat 29:19-20; Shulchan Aruch, O.C. 188:6, 425:3, 487:1, 490:9, 663:2.

[4] Genesis 2:2-3

[5] Rambam, Mishne Torah, Hilchot Shabbat 29:1

[6] See Chapter 3 above, note 6.

[7] This connection between Shabbat and the *Mishkan* is explained by Rabbi Zalman Sorotzkin, Oznaim LaTorah, Exodus 20:10, 25:32, 35:2.

43 | Our Epicenter

Shabbat is contained within the 25-hour experience – but its impact extends beyond that. The character, perspectives and happiness we gain on Shabbat remain with us as we venture out into the week. By placing Shabbat at its epicenter, our entire life is transformed.

Shabbat doesn't stand in isolation. We are called on to *"remember* Shabbat" every day;[1] to place it at the center of our consciousness, allowing its transformative energy to shape every aspect of our lives, embracing its teachings every day.

The way we mark the days of the week reflects this. In Hebrew, the days of the week do not have names, as in English, but are assigned numbers in relation to Shabbat. Sunday is *Yom Rishon* – Day One (from Shabbat). Monday is *Yom Sheini* – Day Two (from Shabbat) – and so on.[2] In this way, we fulfill the special mitzvah to be mindful of Shabbat every day of the week – to "remember the Shabbat day to make it holy."[3] By marking the days in relation to Shabbat, it becomes the center point of each seven-day cycle.

Shabbat influences the week in two directions – as illustrated by a dramatic scenario presented in the Talmud:[4] You're lost in the desert and lose track of time, not even knowing what day of the week it is. When do you mark Shabbat?[5]

IMPACT

The Talmud offers two opinions. One opinion is that on the first day you realize that you have lost track of time, you should mark *that* day as Shabbat. You should then count six days and designate the seventh day as the *following* Shabbat. The other opinion is that from the day you realize that you have lost track of time, you should *first* count six days, and *then* designate the seventh as Shabbat.

The crux of the debate is whether one starts with Shabbat and then counts six days, or counts six days and then marks Shabbat. This debate is premised on the very first Shabbat of history. From Adam and Eve's subjective perspective, they were created on Friday and went straight into Shabbat,[6] and then had six days of work following Shabbat. But when looking at it objectively – from the perspective of the order of Creation – the six days of work came first. Shabbat only followed afterwards.

This debate teaches us[7] that Shabbat influences the week in two ways: it begins the week and elevates the following six days; but it is also the culmination of the week, the apex of the days that build toward it. Shabbat, the center of our week, elevates every day of the week – the days both preceding it and proceeding from it.[8] It stands at the center of the week – and at the epicenter of our lives.

This insight may explain the Divine promise that redemption will come to the world when we keep two Shabbats[9] (not just one[10]). To experience the full power of a Shabbat, we need the cumulative effect of the preceding Shabbat's impact on the week leading up to it. And so, we strive to live from one Shabbat to the next in a virtuous cycle of positivity and light generated by Shabbat, the light increasing with each week that passes.

The centrality of Shabbat and the two directions in which it influences the week is vividly captured by the image of the golden *menorah* in the Temple, with its single central branch surrounded by six other branches, three on each side, each branch tipped with a cup of olive oil feeding a flame.[11] The wicks of the six outer branches were slanted inwards, producing the effect of three flames bent toward the center flame on each side of the menorah.[12] The symbolism is powerful: like the central flame, Shabbat stands at the center of the week, its light flowing into the three days on either side of it, influencing the week in both directions.

This light of Shabbat is reflected in its two inflection points – as Shabbat goes in and as it goes out. We light candles to bring Shabbat in, and we see it out with the fire of the Havdalah candle.[13] With the Friday night candles we celebrate and reaffirm the character, perspectives, and happiness Shabbat brings into our lives. And when we light the Havdalah candle, we rededicate ourselves to infusing the days of the week with this spiritual light, these profound values. This idea is also symbolized by the special meal we have on Saturday night, the melave malka – literally, "accompanying the Queen"[14] – as we take the holiness of Shabbat with us into the week.[15]

Spreading the light of Shabbat is part of our Divine mandate to make our world a better place through our good deeds. Shabbat mirrors the first day of Creation,[16] which begins with God saying: "Let there be light" and ends with God separating light from darkness.[17] Similarly, Shabbat begins with the light of the Shabbat candles, and ends with Havdalah, which literally means distinguishing – marking as separate the light of Shabbat from that of the days of the week.

The Talmud tells us that the light of the first day of Creation was not physical light – the sun and moon and other luminaries were only created on the fourth day[18] – but a spiritual light created as a just reward for the righteous who illuminate the world with their good deeds.[19] By making this the first creation, God shows us that our lives should be guided by the light of His wisdom and commandments. "Let there be light" is thus our clarion call to illuminate the world with our good deeds. We dispel darkness not by confrontation, but by creating more light.[20]

At the beginning of every Shabbat, we reconnect with this Divine light. And at the end of every Shabbat, we carry this light with us into the week ahead.

1 Talmud, Beitza 16a; Midrash, Mechilta D'Rabbi Yishmael 20:8; Ramban, Exodus 20:8; Shulchan Aruch HaGraz 242:10; Mishna Berura 250:2. Shabbat is one of the six things to be remembered daily, see Magen Avraham 60:2; Shulchan Aruch HaGraz 60:4.

2 Midrash, Mechilta D'Rabbi Yishmael 20:8; Aruch HaShulchan, E.H. 126:10. For a deeper insight into this see Shelah, Aseret HaDibrot, Chullin, Torah Ohr 62.

3 Talmud, Beitza 16a, based on Exodus 20:8

4 Talmud, Shabbat 69b

5 The Talmud explains that because any day could be Shabbat, you would have to keep it every day by refraining from all work, except for whatever is necessary to survive. In this way, of course, the days would blend into each other, which is why the Talmud rules that you must still distinguish one day of the week as Shabbat, by reciting Kiddush and Havdalah.

6 Talmud, Sanhedrin 38a

7 This observation is made by Rabbi Avraham Bornsztain, the Sochatchover Rebbe, Avnei Nezer, recorded in Torah Moadim and Likutim, Shabbat, Parshat Vayishlach.

8 See Talmud, Pesachim 106a, with Rashi and Rashbam; Talmud, Gittin 77a. In fact, the halacha teaches that one can make Havdalah until Tuesday afternoon, and then, from Tuesday night, the focus of the week shifts to the coming Shabbat; Talmud, Pesachim 106a; Rambam, Mishne Torah, Hilchot Shabbat 29:4; Shulchan Aruch, O.C. 299:6.

9 Talmud, Shabbat 118b

10 In contrast, see Jerusalem Talmud, Taanit 1:1; Midrash, Shemot Rabba 25:12; Midrash, Tehillim 95:3; Midrash, Yalkut Shimoni on Nach 852.

11 The idea that Shabbat influences the rest of the week, as represented by the structure of the menorah, is presented by Rabbi Yeshayahu HaLevi Horowitz, in Shelah, Aseret HaDibrot, Shabbat, Derech Chaim 2. See also Oznaim LaTorah, Exodus 25:32 for the same idea.

12 Numbers 8:2

13 Shelah, Aseret HaDibrot, Shabbat, Torah Ohr 19

14 Talmud, Shabbat 119b; Rambam, Mishne Torah, Hilchot Shabbat 30:5; Shulchan Aruch, O.C. 300:1

15 Likutei Sichot, Beshalach, vol. 36, sicha 2

Chapter Notes

[16] Shelah, Aseret HaDibrot, Shabbat, Torah Ohr 19

[17] Genesis 1:4-5

[18] Genesis 1:14-19

[19] Talmud, Chagiga 12a; Midrash, Bereishit Rabba 3:6

[20] Chofetz Chaim on the Torah, Genesis 1:3

44 | Our Soulmate

We don't just *keep* Shabbat; we connect deeply with it. Shabbat is our soulmate. And it has been since the beginning of time.

The Midrash expresses this beautifully.[1] It says that when God created the world, each day had a natural partner.[2] Sunday and Wednesday were connected because they had in common the creation of light. Monday and Thursday were connected by being days on which, respectively, the water and the fish, and the skies and the birds, were created.[3] Tuesday and Friday were the days on which land and land animals were created. But Shabbat was created with no partner, and God said: "The Jewish People will be your soulmate."

Like a true soulmate, Shabbat brings us joy and happiness, and also influences us deeply, shaping our character and perspectives, molding our identity. Conversely, divorcing ourselves from Shabbat, our soulmate, means losing a crucial part of Jewish identity.

Every week, when we reconnect with Shabbat, we feel like we have come home to a loving soulmate, our best friend who is always there to hold us and nurture us with love and wisdom – as we sing joyfully at the Friday night table: *Mah Yedidut*,[4] "How beloved a friend is your rest!" We welcome Shabbat into our lives each week with the stirring words of *Lecha Dodi*:[5] "Come, my friend, let us go out to the Bride, let us welcome Shabbat," to reflect the sages of the Talmud who would go out into the fields to welcome Shabbat, which they described as the "Bride."[6]

We reconsecrate our marriage to Shabbat each week.[7] The Hebrew word "Kiddush", our declaration of the sanctity of Shabbat, shares the same root as the word *kiddushin*, which describes the moment when the groom gives his bride a ring at the wedding ceremony, thereby consecrating and formalizing their marriage.[8] When we say Kiddush, we are reconsecrating our bond with Shabbat. On the verse: "Remember the day of Shabbat to sanctify it,"[9] the Midrash says that "remember" refers to the moment that God declared Shabbat to be our soulmate, and that "to sanctify it" means to consecrate Shabbat in marriage.[10]

That bond intensifies over the course of the three stages of Shabbat – Friday night, Shabbat morning and Shabbat afternoon. The three stages of Shabbat – and the Amidah prayers recited at each – reflect the three stages of a wedding ceremony: the sanctification with a ring, the blessings of the *chuppah* (wedding canopy), and *yichud* – the moment of seclusion of the bride and groom just before the celebrations begin.[11]

Just as a true soulmate gives us love and support, holding us and carrying us through life, Shabbat has accompanied us on all our journeys throughout history, across millennia and continents. We have been scattered to every corner of the globe, encountering diverse cultures and languages, an experience that can cause a nation to fragment and then disintegrate. There is no other nation in recorded history that has survived protracted exile and dispersion. Having Shabbat as our constant companion through this turbulence and uncertainty has been vital in helping us defy the odds. It has brought us joy and inspiration, rest and respite, no matter what we have faced.

Like a beloved friend, Shabbat assures us that we are precious and valuable, gently reminding us of our Divine mission, fortifying us with the sense of purpose to endure grueling challenges. Shabbat has given us the courage and strength to withstand all the adversities and adversaries of Jewish history. Shabbat has kept us together.[12]

Shabbat has always been there for us – through times of celebration and mourning, triumph and failure, optimism and despondency. No matter what we have been through, Shabbat has always given us dignity and respite – one day every week when we are free; when we feel blessed.

And the light of Shabbat shines even in our darkest moments. The Talmud[13] says that when the invading soldiers entered the Temple's inner sanctuary to destroy it, they noticed that the golden cherubs were miraculously entwined in a loving embrace, expressing God's love for the people at this terrible moment, on the eve of exile.[14]

It was by Divine decree that the Temple was destroyed, so how could this also be a moment of Divine love?[15] The answer is that it was on Shabbat[16] – the day of Divine love, the day that God's presence is closest to us[17] – that the Holy of Holies was desecrated and destroyed. According to this, the timing of the destruction to coincide with Shabbat was crucial – at the very moment the long exile was beginning, God's presence would be with us in the closest way possible, accompanying us throughout that journey, bringing us strength and comfort, love and support.

Even when we lost everything else – our land, our Jerusalem, our Temple – we could endure because we still had Shabbat.[18] Our eternal soulmate.

Chapter Notes

[1] Midrash, Bereishit Rabba 11:8

[2] Midrash, Bereishit Rabba 11:8, according to the Vilna Gaon. (See, however, Machzor Vitry, Hilchot Shabbat 139.)

[3] See Genesis 1:3-25

[4] See Chapter 37 above, note 4.

[5] See Chapter 37 above, note 5.

[6] Talmud, Shabbat 119a

[7] The ideas in the next few paragraphs are based on the writings of Rabbi Eliyahu ben Shlomo Zalman, the Vilna Gaon, Chidushei Aggadot, Bava Kama 32b. See also Siddur HaGra, Avnei Eliyahu.

[8] See Taz, E.H. 34:2.

[9] Exodus 20:8

[10] See Midrash, Bereishit Rabba 11:8; See also Rabbi Tzvi Hersh Bonhardt, Eretz Tzvi, Ir HaMenucha.

[11] Avudraham, Shabbat Prayers, Evening Service 10; Megaleh Amukot, Parshat Toldot

[12] Kuzari 3:10-11

[13] Talmud, Yoma 54b

[14] This refers to the destruction of the First Temple; see Jerusalem Talmud, Taanit 4:5, which says that the destruction took place on the 1st of Av. That day was Shabbat; see Talmud, Taanit 29a; Talmud, Arachin 11b. Accordingly, the invading soldiers referred to in Talmud, Yoma 54b may have found the actual cherubs that were attached to the Ark of the Covenant. However, according to Rashi, the Talmud is referring to the decorative cherubs on the walls of the Temple. See also Talmud, Yoma 52b, 53b-54a; Talmud, Horayot 12a; Talmud, Keritot 5b.

[15] The ideas in the next few paragraphs are based on Rabbi Yonatan Eybeschutz, Yaarot Devash 13.

[16] Talmud, Taanit 29a; Talmud, Arachin 11b

[17] Zohar 3:179b, as cited in Yaarot Devash 13

[18] See Rabbi Yosef Dov Soloveitchik, Darosh Darash Yosef, Parshat Vayakhel 1: "Shabbat and the Tabernacle," who links this idea to the fact that the building of the Tabernacle was set aside on Shabbat, and that the work that is not allowed on Shabbat is derived from what was needed to construct the Tabernacle.

45 | A Bold Idea

Returning Shabbat to its rightful place at the center of Jewish life is the bold idea we need right now. This has been the driving vision of The Shabbat Project and its thousands of volunteers in communities across the Jewish world.

We need Shabbat now as a matter of personal renewal and national survival – and as the blueprint for a bright future. For it has within it everything we need. It has answers to our most daunting problems. It empowers us to seize the opportunities and confront the challenges we face in these uncertain times.

Modern society is grappling with serious social issues; with high levels of anxiety and discontent, families struggling to connect. We are distracted and overwhelmed by external stimulation and frenetic communication, our lives swamped by unprecedented professional and social demands, our emotional well-being assailed by the frenzy and pressure and pace of modern life.

Our core sense of meaning and clarity of purpose is being eroded by a noisy and confusing world, with a cacophony of confident voices peddling every philosophy and product imaginable. The seismic political, technological and socio-economic changes that regularly shake the foundations of society make our world feel more unstable than ever.

IMPACT

Amid this turbulence and relentless pressure, Shabbat gives us the time and space we need to breathe, to create ourselves – to build our inner world, strengthen our faith, nurture our family, and find meaning and purpose; to create a better quality of life. It is the "source of all blessing,"[1] the Divine gift[2] of a day of happiness and togetherness with a formula to curate the kind of life we yearn for, a refreshing source of renewal never more than a few days away.

Shabbat instills in us the humility, wisdom, trust, optimism, generosity, idealism, gentleness, appreciation, and stillness we need to thrive, psychologically, ethically, spiritually; all the character traits we need to live optimally and joyfully. It guides us to renew ourselves and nurture our most precious relationships, to make the most of our time, to find wholeness in our lives.

It teaches us the skills and lessons of happiness from our Creator, Who knows us better than we know ourselves. It inspires us to savor life's blessings, to free ourselves from our burdens, to access true pleasure, to live holistically.

Shabbat is the voice of clarity and purpose we need in this confusing world. Every week it reminds us of the Divine values and perspectives that have guided generations of Jews across continents and historical eras.

In doing so, Shabbat addresses the most serious existential threat to the future of the Jewish People – assimilation rooted in apathy, ignorance, and disengagement. At its heart, this problem is an identity crisis. It is the fundamental question of 'why be Jewish?' We need to show a new generation of Jews why being Jewish is something they would want for themselves. The only way to do this is to ensure that Jewish identity is not defined by the hatred and persecution of others, but by the nobility and beauty of our mission – by our higher meaning and purpose.

Shabbat provides compelling answers to 'why be Jewish?' It teaches us that we have a Creator and that He cares about us; that we are God's partners in creating a better world; that our lives have purpose, and that our good deeds connect us to Him and to the people around us. It teaches us that this world is not the end – that there is another, eternal world; but also that everything we need to accomplish, we need to accomplish in *this* world, lending an urgency and purpose to our existence here on earth and helping us realize the preciousness of every moment of our lives. It teaches us the power and purpose of Jewish destiny, and how it is intertwined with the ultimate destination of all humanity in a redeemed world.

The only true answer to apathy and assimilation is to understand *why* we should be Jewish in the first place. Without such an understanding, we will not be able to convince the next generation of Jews why they should not abandon their heritage; why they should not take the path of least resistance and assimilate. Shabbat empowers us to impart this understanding.

In the Diaspora, Shabbat is our greatest buffer against assimilation. History has demonstrated that when Jews abandon Shabbat, their descendants eventually disappear as Jews. And in Israel, Shabbat has the power to reinspire a new generation of Israelis with national pride, rooted in a renewed sense of the historic importance and nobility of the Jewish mission. Shabbat gives us the values and vision we need to chart our path forward with confidence and purpose.

But, as we have explored in these pages, we can only access the remarkable gifts of Shabbat when we adhere to its original Divine formula. For more than 3,300 years, the vast majority of Jews kept Shabbat in full accordance with the *halacha*. We kept it with tenacity, loyalty, and love befitting our eternal soulmate. But over the last century, our connection to the full Shabbat experience has been so weakened that now most Jews do not keep it. This is a historical anomaly. We must reverse that.

It is time for us to return to the bold idea of a fully immersive 25-hour Shabbat, kept with all its *halachic* detail, because therein lies its real power. When diluted or cut short or denuded of its Divine intent, it loses its potential to change us and to change the Jewish world. Reduced to a one-dimensional cultural activity or list of arbitrary restrictions, Shabbat is shorn of its spiritual depth and beauty. Regarded merely as the Jewish weekend, Shabbat loses its power and uniqueness. And even for those who keep Shabbat already, let it not be by rote and habit – let it instead be the fully transformative experience it is designed to be.

For Shabbat is not merely an abstract concept, an intellectual construct. It is an immersive, lived experience as shaped by the *halacha*. The philosophy of Shabbat is inseparable from the practical aspects of the day. The ideas animate our actions. And our actions bring these ideas to life. It is the Divine blueprint of the day, as sketched by the *halacha*, that makes it so revolutionary.

Shabbat is the bold idea we need now, to realize a vibrant and bright Jewish future. It is our spiritual birthright, and now is the time to claim it, fully. Shabbat has the power to redeem us, personally and nationally. It is God's gift to us all. Our sages of the Talmud, drawing on the oral tradition received at Sinai, tell us that Shabbat is the gateway to redemption.[3] It redeems us by transforming us – building our character, shaping our perspectives, enabling us to create ourselves. It redeems us by creating a stronger, more vibrant, more bountiful Jewish world.

And it redeems us with its spiritual power to bring the Final Redemption to our world, to usher in the time when all the Divine promises, described so movingly by Isaiah, will be fulfilled:

"Comfort, comfort My people... speak to the heart of Jerusalem and proclaim to her that her time [of exile] has been completed[4]... from Zion will the Torah come forth, and the word of God from Jerusalem... they shall beat their swords into plowshares and their spears into pruning hooks; nation will not lift up sword against nation, neither will they learn war anymore[5]... the earth will be filled with the knowledge of God as the waters cover the oceans."[6]

Chapter Notes

[1] The phrase "the source of blessing", well known from Lecha Dodi (see Chapter 37 above, note 5), is based on earlier sources. The Zohar 2:63b states explicitly, "All the days of the week are blessed through Shabbat." See Genesis 2:3 with Ramban and Rabbeinu Bechaye. See also Proverbs 10:22, "The blessing of God makes one rich," which refers to Shabbat: Jerusalem Talmud Berachot 2:7; Jerusalem Talmud Moed Katan 3:5; Bereishit Rabba 11:1; Pesikta Rabbati 46:1. In addition, see Talmud, Shabbat 118a and 119a.

[2] See Chapter 32 above, note 3.

[3] Jerusalem Talmud, Taanit 1:1; Talmud, Shabbat 118b. These statements of the Talmud are classically interpreted to refer to the idea that the merit of the entire Jewish People keeping Shabbat can usher in the Final Redemption. This paragraph relies on reading the promise of redemption more broadly.

[4] Isaiah 40:1-2

[5] Isaiah 2:3-4; see also Micah 4:2-3; Joel 4:10

[6] Isaiah 11:9; see also Habakkuk 2:14

AFTERWORD

The Unexpected Story of The Shabbat Project

The Unexpected Story of
the Shabbat Project

The Shabbat Project demonstrates vividly the power of Shabbat in action. I share with you its story here because it brings to life the ideas about Shabbat expressed in this book. It shows the resilience of the unbreakable bond, spanning thousands of years, between the Jewish people and Shabbat. It shows how Shabbat bridges divides, inspiring, energizing, and uplifting all Jews no matter their background, culture, or level of observance. It shows how Shabbat, with its Divine gifts of self-creation and happiness, is compelling for us today.

—

The Shabbat Project surprised me from the start. Its unexpected story begins in early 2013, when I first remember discussing the idea with my wife, Gina. A call for the entire South African Jewish community, regardless of background, affiliation or level of observance, to keep a full 25-hour Shabbat together. We were not sure it was going to work; we thought perhaps it was asking too much.

When we broached the idea with colleagues and friends, people were understandably skeptical. Many thought we should instead suggest keeping one aspect of Shabbat rather than the whole thing. Very few thought it was likely to succeed.

We decided to go ahead anyway. I remember Gina saying that even if just a few people would keep Shabbat for the first time, it would be worth it.

We launched the project in June. We didn't really have much of a plan.

What we did have was a date, and a rallying call of "Keeping It Together." We scheduled The Shabbat Project for 11/12 October, and a few weeks after the launch, we released what has become its guiding manifesto:

1. *Together we will keep this Shabbat from sundown to stars out.*

2. *We will keep it in its entirety, in all its halachic detail and splendor as it has been kept throughout the ages.*

3. *Its rhythm will unite us with each other, with Jews around the world and throughout the ages.*

4. *On this day we will create a warm and loving space, holding our families together.*

5. *On this day we will lay down the burdens, distractions, demands and pressures of daily life.*

6. *On this day we will renew ourselves, emerging spiritually, emotionally, and physically invigorated.*

7. *On this day we will own our precious heritage, wearing it as a badge of pride and honor.*

8. *Together we embark on this great adventure to rediscover our God-given gift of Shabbat.*

We then released Gina's "Unofficial Guide to Keeping it Together" to help people understand the practicalities of keeping Shabbat.

We also released a Shabbat "toolkit", giving people a better understanding of all the various Shabbat traditions and experiences.

We had no idea where this was going to end up.

—

And then the magic started. Right from the beginning, the unusual, supernatural connection between the Jewish People and Shabbat was evident. It seems unlikely even now, but almost overnight The Shabbat Project took on a life of its own.

We began by approaching different people in the community to get on board and commit to "keeping it together" that Shabbat. And we had the most unusual and unexpected reactions.

I remember a conversation I had with one of South Africa's Jewish pop stars, Danny K. I phoned him up to ask him, would he keep that Shabbat? And would he be prepared to make a video calling on others to do so? He said he supported the idea in principle, but unfortunately, he had a concert planned for that very Friday night. He said he would think about it. A few days later, Danny called me to say that he had changed his mind. He would reschedule the concert, block off that Shabbat in his calendar, and encourage others to do the same.

Nik Rabinowitz, one of South Africa's best loved comedians, followed suit. Soon there were hundreds of videos of people from the community – business leaders, high school learners, communal leaders, celebrities, and everyone in between – all committing to 'keeping it together'.

These videos were viewed and shared via Facebook, and other platforms, which changed the dynamic of how the message spread – instead of top-down it moved quickly and organically from one friend to another, igniting a grassroots movement.

Through the power of social media, the medium became the message – a sense that Shabbat (and this initiative) belonged to everyone; that we were all equal partners in this exciting and meaningful endeavor.

A natural momentum took hold as people rallied behind the idea of celebrating and keeping one Shabbat in full, together. The concept caught fire. There was a sense of people not wanting to be left out. There came a point when the question wasn't who was going to participate in The Shabbat Project, but who wasn't.

Friends got together to organize huge "street dinners." People keeping Shabbat for the first time were inviting friends and neighbors for Shabbat meals in their gardens. Shabbat classes and courses were being rolled out across the community.

I will never forget the first challah bake. Though the challah bake has become iconically connected to The Shabbat Project, the idea sprang from nowhere. It was never part of the original plan, which was simply to keep Shabbat. It was a spur-of-the-moment idea just a few days before the big Shabbat: an open invitation to gather together to make challah on the streets of Johannesburg.

Again, we could just feel events orchestrated by a Divine Hand. Beloved Israeli educator and speaker Rabbanit Yemima Mizrachi, who would lead the first challah bake, "just happened" to be in Johannesburg at the time. So, too, musician Shlomo Katz. And mothers and daughters came pouring onto the streets for that first challah bake in their thousands, as people were swept up in the emotion and excitement of the experience.

This momentum continued into Shabbat.

South Africa's arena-sized synagogues reported capacity turn-outs – crowds exceeding those of Kol Nidrei and first night Rosh Hashana – and empty parking lots. Hundreds of residents of

Oaklands, Johannesburg, gathered together in the streets of the suburb for a Friday night "dinner under the stars."

In the beach-side suburb of Camps Bay in Cape Town, one family had 30 guests around their Shabbat lunch table who were keeping Shabbat for the first time. Another Johannesburg family hosted a high school reunion with a difference, as around 50 former classmates gathered as guests in their home to keep Shabbat together. A Grade 9 pupil at King David Linksfield, South Africa's largest Jewish day school, said he couldn't think of a single one of his peers who wasn't keeping that Shabbat. There were reports of empty hairdressing salons and golf clubs, of soccer coaches wondering where all the kids had gone.

The majority of South Africa's Jews kept that Shabbat in full. And as the stars came out on 12 October, jubilant scenes erupted as thousands gathered at open-air Havdalah concerts in Johannesburg and Cape Town, giving expression to their feelings in the most fitting way possible – through song and dance.

We were astounded at how the entire community got on board. The spirit was overwhelming; the excitement, the sense of joy and celebration. And the ease with which everything happened. It all seemed so natural and spontaneous. People were fully open to the experience from the beginning.

Straight after Shabbat, participants shared their photos from the challah bake and Havdalah concerts, and of their Shabbat preparations, on social media. These posts went viral. Soon people were writing in from around the world, eager to bring The Shabbat Project to their own cities and communities.

—

AFTERWORD

At this point we had to figure out what to do. There had certainly never been any intention to take this global. And yet the need seemed to spring naturally from the ground.

Seeing the results of a survey conducted among South African Jews a few weeks after the project – 90% of respondents indicated that, going forward, they would like to keep more of Shabbat – made it even clearer to us. If there was a hunger in South Africa, we reasoned, there was a hunger elsewhere, too. From the heartfelt messages we'd received from around the world, it seemed the project had tapped into something deep within the hearts and souls of Jews everywhere.

We released a video documenting what happened in South Africa and announced a date for the inaugural international Shabbat Project: 24/25 October 2014. In essence, it was an invitation to world Jewry to join South African Jews to keep one 25-hour Shabbat, based on the optimistic belief that what happened in one community could happen everywhere.

We published the video on YouTube in March just before Purim – and then the floodgates opened. Hundreds of emails poured in from every corner of the globe, from people wanting to participate in The Shabbat Project. Within a matter of months, we had volunteers working to bring The Shabbat Project to their communities in more than 460 cities and 64 countries, across multiple languages – English, Hebrew, French, Spanish, Russian, German, Portuguese.

In Johannesburg, a team of designers, copywriters and strategists, led by Laurence Horwitz, the creative director who had masterminded the original marketing campaign in the first year of the project, worked around the clock to custom-design materials for literally hundreds of cities, while project manager, Rosy Hollander, tirelessly coordinated logistics with volunteers across the globe.

I'd never seen anything like it. I witnessed the power of Shabbat to break through all the barriers and differences that seem to separate us – barriers of language and culture, differences in ideological outlook and levels of religious observance.

In 2015, The Shabbat Project doubled in size, reaching 918 cities and 84 countries. The expansion was supported by an international call center in Tel Aviv, where Tanya Harati, a project manager who had recently made aliyah from South Africa, expertly directed a team manning partner desks, assisting thousands of partners all over the world across 10 different languages.

By 2019, the project had grown to more than 1,600 cities and 100 countries. An untold number have observed Shabbat in full for the first time in their lives.

And every step of the way it has had a natural energy. All we've had to do is guide it. In every city, in every community, it has needed nothing more than a little support for people to take ownership of it. We've provided our partners around the world with marketing collateral and educational material, and Shabbat has done the rest.

I've come to realize that it's not something rational – this intense connection between Jews and Shabbat; that it's something deep in our psyche, something ingrained in our identity, something woven into our souls.

—

I have seen Shabbat inspire people to become leaders. An army of 5,000 volunteers has sprung up to drive this project throughout the world – people so moved by their connection to Shabbat they feel compelled to share it with others, uniting their communities around this mitzvah. The work they've done has been truly awe-inspiring.

These Shabbat activists have brought the project, with unique flavor and style, to cities throughout the globe. Thanks to their efforts, in LA and London, Melbourne and Moscow, Buenos Aires and Berlin, Tel Aviv and Tokyo, Manila and Montreal, Addis Ababa and Ashkelon, Sao Paulo and Strasbourg, and everywhere in between – Jews from all walks of life, of all levels of observance, have united to observe a full Shabbat together.

Through initiatives big and small, our volunteer partners have inspired entire communities. They have put together events on a grand scale – mass city-wide spectacles and logistics-defying Shabbat banquets that have drawn crowds in their thousands: a remarkable musical Kabbalat Shabbat service on Sydney's Bondi Beach; a Shabbat dinner for students hosted by the Sigma Chi fraternity house at the University of Southern California (USC) – the "largest Jewish event ever held at USC" according to the university's newspaper; a Havdalah concert in a city park adjoining the Buenos Aires planetarium, organized with the support of the municipality of Buenos Aires; a challah bake at the Baltimore Convention Center covered by ABC News; a Shabbat dinner on the streets of LA's Pico Boulevard, with guests at 300 tables stretching five Los Angeles city blocks, billed as the biggest in history.

Just as importantly, these intrepid volunteers have originated innovative ideas that have kept The Shabbat Project fresh and exciting, year after year. From a Yoga Retreat in Rockland County to a Glow in the Dark Challah Bake in Costa Rica; from a Cruise Line Shabbaton in the middle of the Atlantic Ocean to a Shabbat on the slopes of Mount Kilimanjaro; from a Shabbat dinner held in a shipping container at Tel Aviv Port to a Seudah Shlishit in a bar in central Jerusalem. Pop-up shuls, street dinners, glamping, couch-surfing, and so much more.

Scores of trailblazing Shabbat Project "city captains" have come to the fore, galvanizing entire communities.

Among them, Emilio Penhos, a prominent business and community leader in Mexico City, has helped coordinate events that in some years have reached up to 15,000 Jews in the community – among them, Shabbatons held at city hotels to make it easier for people to keep Shabbat, and a Shabbaton at a local school gymnasium where 260 members of Tnua, a secular youth movement, kept Shabbat together. In Nice, France, Dafna Benizri – a mother of four and grandmother of seven, and a former kindergarten teacher and hotel manager – has run numerous oversubscribed Shabbat Project events each year, including a series of glittering ballroom banquets on the famous Promenade des Anglais.

In Panama City, Daniela Lowinger has helped establish the city as a hub of the project with initiatives such as a program involving thousands of learners from the city's Jewish day schools, incorporating Shabbat-themed activities and learning modules into the school curriculum. In Arizona, Robin Meyerson, a speaker, author and life coach, has run events including a novel "Shabbat Shuk", a remarkably inclusive challah bake and, most recently, a "12-week Shabbat challenge," which have become an incredible "gateway" experience for many.

—

I have seen Shabbat move not only big, bustling Jewish communities, but also Jews in far-flung places with no Jewish infrastructure, no community around for support, and very little connection to anything Jewish.

Conway, Arkansas is a rural city in the heart of rural America, home to around 60,000 people, with fewer than 10 Jews. One of them is Abir Schweizer, who wrote to me to share his pain of feeling alone as a Jew, and what it meant to him to feel part of a "global Jewish family" keeping it together – that "you can never feel alone on a Shabbos like this."

Faisel "Fischel" Benkhald may be one of the only living Jews in Karachi, Pakistan. Though his mother is Jewish, he was officially registered as a Muslim since apostasy is theoretically punishable by death. Faisel found out about The Shabbat Project on Twitter, and contacted the head office. I spoke to him over the phone about his situation and encouraged him to participate. He told me there are other Jews in hiding in the country who are registered as Muslims. During the 2016 Shabbat Project, he kept Shabbat for the first time, with Jews around the world. Soon after, he changed his status to Jewish, even at the risk of his own life.

Ruti Madar, living in Honolulu, Hawaii, said there was a Chabad on the island, but it was more than an hour's walk from her house, so she and her family tended to stay home alone on Shabbat. She wrote in to say how The Shabbat Project gave her the impetus to change that and reach out to other Jews on the island.

Daniel Hecht is a doctor who lived alone in the Swedish countryside, almost 150 miles away from the nearest synagogue in Stockholm. During the 2017 Shabbat Project, he felt like he was "celebrating Shabbat with a very big family." He has since moved to Stockholm to be part of a Jewish community.

In 2016, Zvi Gleiberman was studying at a university in The Bottom, a town on the island of Saba in the Eastern Caribbean Islands. Surprisingly, Zvi was not the only Jewish student studying on this remote island. With The Shabbat Project as the backdrop, he hosted a four-course Friday night dinner at his apartment for his fellow Jewish medical students – toasting, along with his friends, their fellow Jews on six continents "keeping it together."

Then there were the Jewish soldiers stationed on the Coalition Military Base in northern Iraq, who felt it was "just so cool to reflect on the fact that here in Iraq, we joined Jews around the world celebrating this Shabbat together."

Stories emerged of people keeping it together in even more remote places: in Amman, Jordan; in Lima, Peru; in Srirangapatna; India; in Maputo, Mozambique; on an island in the Outer Hebrides.

There are stories that simply took my breath away. A large group of students attended a Shabbat dinner in Izmir, Turkey; Swaziland's entire Jewish community, comprising 18 families, gathered for a communal Shabbat meal at someone's home, endeavoring to keep Shabbat in full; the Griqualand West Hebrew Congregation in South Africa's Karoo desert held a Shabbat morning service for the first time in years; two dozen Jews participated in a Shabbaton at a local hostel in downtown Mumbai; another Shabbaton in Ajaccio, Corsica, drew 40 participants – and there are "officially" no Jews in Corsica according to a national register.

But the story that has perhaps moved me most came from a town called Fernley, deep in the Nevada desert. It's a story that aptly illustrates both the power of a people's movement driven by passionate volunteers, and the power of Shabbat to bring Jews together and connect them with their heritage.

Keli Rae is a doting grandmother who had emigrated to Fernley from Sydney to be near her family, who had moved there for work. They were so isolated that one day her granddaughter asked her: "Bubbie, are there any other Jews in the world?" For The Shabbat Project, Keli decided to send out an open invitation to Shabbat dinner at her house – and showed her granddaughter that there were even Jews in Fernley...

I put the word out on local Fernley Facebook groups. In the first 24 hours, six Jewish families responded. None had any real prior affiliation with Judaism.

My granddaughter and I got to work with the preparation. Together, we made up bags with candles and matches, and I printed out transliterated Hebrew-English sheets of the brachot for candle-lighting and for hand-washing and Hamotzi. On Monday morning, we traveled to Trader Joe's in Reno (about 40 miles away) to stock up on kosher chickens.

I cleared some space in the living room, and asked a few of the guests to bring extra chairs. Aside from the chairs, two of them brought family heirloom Kiddush cups and one had an embroidered Shabbat tablecloth that someone in her family had made. We asked the women if they wished to light candles and they eagerly agreed to. They especially liked seeing my other one-year-old granddaughter cover her eyes when anyone repeated the bracha ...

—

Through The Shabbat Project, I have seen how the pull of Shabbat is so powerful it draws Jews in places where decades of government oppression all but uprooted Judaism. But the eternal bond with Shabbat can never be broken. Consider the remarkable scenes in Pinsk in 2017, where 300 Belarusians from across the country attended a full Shabbaton for The Shabbat Project that year. For many, this wasn't just their first Shabbat – it was their first Jewish experience. Amid tears and high emotions, three sets of parents made the snap decision to enroll their children at Pinsk's Jewish school.

I was so moved to read Rabbi Moshe Fhima's account of the event:

It was after 11:30pm – already five hours after Shabbos was over – and three women were sitting alone in the dining room, crying. After one of the organizers approached them, they explained that they did not want the emotions and experience that they had from their first Shabbos in their lives to diminish.

Preparations for the Pinsk Shabbaton literally only began a week before the event, once funding for the event had been secured. A car was sent out to Moscow (15 hours in the snow in each direction) to buy chickens for Shabbos and a small advertisement was posted on our website. Within 24 hours we had more than 300 spaces filled.

People came from all over the country – some even traveled 16 hours by train in each direction.

The Shabbos weekend began with the local mothers and grandmothers preparing challah on Thursday night with the help of the girls of The Beis Aharon School. Communism had torn two generations away from anything even slightly connected to Yiddishkeit, and so Jewish education in Belarus has typically not been passed from mother to daughter but vice versa. To see Holocaust survivors preparing challah for the very first time after all their years of suffering was a truly emotional sight.

Throughout the Shabbos, guests enjoyed interesting shiurim on various Jewish topics, giving them a taste for Judaism and inspiring them to want to know more. The children of the school sang zemiros (Shabbat songs) as well as the famous "Ribbon Ha'olamim" in Russian. The effect of these experiences will be felt for many months. Three parents enrolled their children into the schools immediately after

Shabbos. They wanted their children to have the opportunity they never had – to grow up like regular Jews. These children were so far from anything that they did not even have a bris, or know Alef Beis, or know what kosher food was. And they'd certainly never kept a Shabbos.

Scores of towns in Belarus, Ukraine and Lithuania that once bustled with Jewish life before the Holocaust have had a Shabbat-inspired reawakening. Places where Judaism had been crushed by the Soviet regime. And yet this spiritual connection to Shabbat was simply beneath the surface, waiting to be rekindled.

And I saw the same Shabbat spark among Jews who had lost their connection in an open, free society. Lana Wilder from Arizona was an unaffiliated, secular Jew married to an unaffiliated non-Jew. A friend convinced her to attend a Shabbat Project challah bake in 2014, and that set her on a life-changing journey, which she shared with me:

When I walked into the room at the JCC, I was overwhelmed by a feeling of awe; by the spirit and presence of hundreds of Jewish women from all walks of life. It literally sent shivers down my spine. I felt pride and awe and an overwhelming sense of love. And at that moment I realized that I had the obligation to maintain that 4,000-year-old chain connecting my children back through Sinai to Sarah and the other matriarchs.

My husband, Chris and I decided to participate in the whole Shabbat Project experience that year. We were invited to a community dinner and Shabbat lunch. We walked to shul, and attended my husband's first service. We kept Shabbat and we have never looked back.

Today, I bake challah every week with my daughter. My husband and I kashered our kitchen and have kept Shabbat every week since that fateful day in 2014. Chris recently completed his conversion through the Beth Din.

Similarly, Ilana Panush from Plano, Texas wrote to us to share how moved she was by her Shabbat experience:

Six years ago, my family decided to join The Shabbos Project. We had never before kept Shabbos. After the 25 hours were over, I had such a great feeling. We participated again the following year, and for some reason I felt even better. The year after that, we moved to a new residence within the Plano eruv and within walking distance of shul so we could keep Shabbos. I would like to thank everyone who showed us what Shabbos is all about.

Shabbat connects with Jews no matter how far they have drifted. One story that has stuck with me was how, in 2014, ten Jewish girls from Miami's Palmer Trinity episcopal school in Miami were among a crowd of 5,000 women at the Miami challah bake. The organizers told us it was the first exposure these girls had ever had to anything Jewish.

Shabbat has the power to connect with Jews who didn't even know they were Jewish. After the first Shabbat Project in South Africa, I received a letter from Tamryn Scheepers, a purportedly Christian woman who taught Afrikaans and Physical Education at a local Jewish day school. In her role at the school, she had found out about The Shabbat Project, and had decided to give it a try, participating in the challah bake, attending shul on Friday night with a Jewish colleague, and even keeping Shabbat. She said the experience had left her feeling "rejuvenated and full of life" and described it as an "amazing spiritual journey." As I read her email, I discovered something that gave me shivers. Here is what Tamryn shared:

AFTERWORD

> *My [maternal] grandmother was born during World War II near Calais in northern France. Her mother's family was Jewish (their surname was Isaac), but because of the German occupation of France, they could not announce their religion, and my grandmother was brought up as a Catholic...*

Afterwards, Tamryn told me that she had since become aware that in *halachic* terms she is Jewish. She and her mother were inspired and excited to continue the journey of rediscovering their Jewish heritage.

—

Most heartwarmingly, I have seen the power of Shabbat to unify. A wonderful story emerged involving two communities in Gateshead and Newcastle with little in common – separated by a river but also by a hundred years of history. Gateshead resident Yonni Klajn describes how, through Shabbat, they were brought together:

> *This past Shabbos afternoon, history was made. Not just because fifty people from Gateshead gave up their sacrosanct Shabbos shluff (sleep), but because they did it to walk for over an hour, crossing the River Tyne to join the Newcastle community for mincha (the afternoon prayer service) and seuda shlishis (the third meal). The atmosphere was electric. We mingled and even danced together. Both communities were left tremendously uplifted. Ultimately, this idea that all Jews should keep Shabbos wherever they are in the world was a catalyst for another achievement: the uniting of our two communities.*

Daniel Cohen, then a 19-year-old college student, who led The Shabbat Project in Seattle in 2015, told me:

So much of the Seattle community lives in its own little world – the Orthodox keep to themselves, the Reform and Conservative communities keep to themselves, and nobody really knows each other, so nobody really communicates. This was the perfect opportunity for our community to unite under the banner of Jewish pride. Under the banner of Shabbat.

Ilana Chilewitz, a volunteer from Toronto, co-chaired the city's very first Shabbat Project. She described to me their weekly planning meetings leading up to the project:

The meetings were electrifying. It was incredible to be sitting at a table with representatives from organizations such as Chabad, NCSY, Aish Hatorah, and all different denominations. So many passionate individuals who want to make a difference in any way they can. One member of the team put it beautifully – 'when we come into a Shabbat Project meeting, we leave our hats at the door.' Before the weekend of The Shabbat Project even began, the unity in Toronto was palpable.

Rabbi Moshe Kahn, a Chabad youth rabbi and director in Melbourne who helped head up The Shabbat Project in the city, noted how there is "no competition, everyone is a part of The Shabbat Project. This is something that's larger than any individual or any individual organization. At our last committee meeting, I took a moment to look around the room at the diversity of our committee members and I got goosebumps."

At a Havdalah concert in Mexico, the Maccabeats, who were performing on the night, said they had never played a concert where different denominations were seated together.

In San Diego, the *San Diego Tribune* called the city's Shabbat Project celebrations – in which close to 20,000 people partici-pated among a Jewish population of whom just 17% are affiliated and 3% Orthodox – "miraculous."

AFTERWORD

Through the power of Shabbat, the project has brought together demographics that would otherwise not have anything to do with each other. Nowhere has this been more evident than in Israel.

I recall when the first Israeli volunteers embarked on bringing The Shabbat Project to their communities, there was a lot of skepticism. The prevailing belief was that Shabbat was a touch-point of the culture war in Israel between religious and secular; that Israel was an intense, acrimonious environment in which to introduce the The Shabbat Project. And yet, over the years, I have witnessed Israel defy these concerns, as summed up so beautifully by Robby Nissan, a creative executive who played an important part in the first few years of the project:

> We extended a handshake to Israeli society and we got a hug in return. It has made me realize that in every Jew, there is a deep yearning to be part of the history and the heritage, to connect to the sacred traditions that make us Jewish. And who doesn't want one day of relief from the rat race and the screens to focus on family and community? The Shabbat Project has effectively laid the foundation for a bridge between two worlds.

I've witnessed this "bridge between two worlds" on so many occasions in Israel. I remember visiting the Ramat David Air Force Base, home to one of the most elite units in the country, and hearing about their experiences – how, in the words of one of the pilots, Yosi Levi, they "made Kiddush and shared dinner and sang Shabbat songs together as a community for the first time... it gave us a shiver."

Orit Messer-Harel helped coordinate those celebrations in Ramat David, and elsewhere in the Emek Yizre'el region whose farming communities, despite being overwhelmingly secular, have been enthusiastic participants. In a meeting with Orit, I asked what motivated her – by her own admission "traditional" rather than observant – to champion The Shabbat Project. She said it gave her great happiness to bring Jews together and help them reconnect with Judaism through Shabbat. Movingly, she told me: "Somewhere along the way, some of us Jews have lost who we are. Through our politics and our divisions and our petty arguments, we've lost what makes us special as a people, what makes us *Jewish*. But Shabbat can help us find it again."

And this has been the story in countless communities across Israel. Yair Gutman lives in the small village of Elyachin in northern Israel. The community is highly stratified along religious lines, living in the same town though not often coming into meaningful contact with one another. He relates how a Shabbat Project event brought the community together again.

We had a Friday night Ja'ala – a traditional Yemenite after-dinner gathering where people sit together in small circles, talking and, of course, snacking. Unobservant, Haredi, religious Zionists – everyone sat together in these mixed circles and talked about how the community used to be more together and how, in recent years, the differences have become more emphasized. And yet this gathering gave people a real sense of togetherness, which doesn't happen very often. What was especially inspiring was how our two youth movements with very different political and religious ideologies – Bnei Akiva and Hamoshavim – held a joint activity about tolerance and unity. I saw how The Shabbat Project touches everyone.

Etti Cohen from Bnei Ayish in central Israel recalls similarly charged scenes in her *yishuv*.

We had an amazing, highly emotional Shabbat, and people literally shed tears. Nearly 400 people took part in the event held on the main road of the yishuv. The participants were young and old. Elderly Holocaust survivors and senior citizens mixed with children. Observant Jews joined with non-observant Jews. Everyone sat in silence when the rabbi of the yishuv said Kiddush. Tears streamed from a group of women who, for nearly 30 years, had not heard Kiddush and had not experienced an atmosphere and a group of Jews like on this holy day. A Holocaust survivor was completely overcome with emotion. The event left no one untouched.

In Eilat, Aharon Ackerman co-opted the city's municipality, running programs in city parks, special school events, and mass, open-invitation Shabbat dinners. In 2021, at one such dinner for 400 people held on a football field in the Shahamon district of Eilat, the city's secular mayor, Eli Lankri, got up to speak and, rather than reciting the usual platitudes, remarked how The Shabbat Project was "bringing unity and holiness to Eilat."

There is one particular group of partners who symbolize this promise of a more unified Israeli society through the healing power of Shabbat. They are called Mothers with Meaning. This group of volunteer moms, of all levels of observance, led by "Chief Mom" Chani Sternlicht, make it their mission to effect broad social change in Israel through Jewish values, and have run scores of events in towns and cities across the country; places like Kochav Yair, for example, on the outskirts of Kfar Saba.

Shikma Kisar, a volunteer for Mothers with Meaning, described a Shabbat Project event held there:

We set out a Friday night Kiddush on 30 neighborhood streets. Old neighbors and new... people of different religious backgrounds... young and old... all came together. So many different people, all of them smiling, happy, ready to feel the closeness and the togetherness of a Shabbat celebrated in a spirit of unity. Tensions evaporated; long-standing anger that had simmered over decades suddenly disappeared over the course of a single Shabbat. A Shabbat of reconciliation and love. A Shabbat of healing.

I've seen this healing power of Shabbat in Israel through the project in so many guises: in the amazing White City Shabbat Tel Aviv events that have attracted thousands; in how HaTzofim, Israel's biggest secular youth movement, sent out thousands of their young scouts to organize community events and Shabbatonim across Israel, working hand-in-hand with the religious Bnei Akiva youth movement; in the way the educational division of the IDF sent dedicated material about Shabbat to army bases across the country, and commanders at these bases addressed their troops about the importance of Shabbat and of Jewish unity; in the manner in which city mayors and local municipalities have given their all to driving the project in their cities, from Ashkelon in the south to Afula in the north; in how Sderot has run The Shabbat Project under fire; and how Carmiel and Netanya and Ashdod, and more than 50 other towns, distributed Shabbat packages in the middle of the coronavirus pandemic.

—

I've also seen the power of Shabbat to connect with Jews and unify us through the most unlikely alliance of public figures who have come out in support of the project: from Rabbi Chaim Kanievsky zt'l to political leaders from across the ideological spectrum – Prime Ministers Benjamin Netanyahu, Naftali Bennet and Yair Lapid; as well as President Reuven Rivlin. President Isaac Herzog's support for The Shabbat Project came through first in his role as chairman of the Jewish Agency, and now as the 11th head of state, through his generous endorsements and open public support, describing the project as something that "touches our collective souls."

Then there are famous actors and musicians in Israel like Shlomi Shabbat – who told me that he would not perform a concert on Shabbat on principle – and Aviv Alush, who, in a moving video message, said:

> *A worldwide Shabbat that all of us keep together – observant, not observant, less connected, more connected. I think there's something so beautiful and unifying in it. Personally, I first encountered The Shabbat Project three years ago and I remember telling my wife, 'Yalla, let's give it a shot, what do we have to lose?' And it was just a magical experience – the family bonding, the quiet, the disconnecting. Just one Shabbat, together.*

Natan Sharansky has been another key ally. He understands the life-giving power of Shabbat from his days imprisoned in a Soviet Gulag; and in his capacity as head of the Jewish Agency, he harnessed the agency's vast network to promote The Shabbat Project worldwide.

And countless other public figures worldwide have got behind the project. Senator Joe Lieberman – who was a handful of votes away from becoming America's first Jewish vice-president, and whose commitment to keeping Shabbat in the highest corridors of power is legendary – is a member of The Shabbat Project's advisory board, alongside Sharansky.

Professor Dan Ariely, the Duke University professor of psychology and behavioral economics – who, in the course of a conversation we had in Johannesburg in 2013, sparked some of the ideas that led to the conception of The Shabbat Project – has spoken often about the psychological benefits of Shabbat and how it resonates with deep human needs.

Alexandre Elicha, co-founder and creative director of the famous Kooples fashion house, who kept his first Shabbat on the island of Ibiza, of all places, told his story on video so that we could share it with all our Shabbat Project participants.

Paula Abdul, the multi-award-winning US entertainer, released a video calling for people to keep Shabbat for the project, which was carried on national television in Israel.

Mayim Bialik, the popular Emmy-nominated actress and accomplished film director (and also a neuroscientist), called on her legions of fans around the world to "try one Shabbat."

Joining this amazing international alliance in promoting The Shabbat Project in their personal capacity are international welterweight boxing champion, Dmitry Salita; singer-songwriter, Alex Clare; best-selling crime thriller author, Faye Kellerman; Nobel prize-winning biologist, Aaron Ciechanover; Nobel-prize winning mathematician, Robert Aumann; and many others.

What unites such an eclectic group – a Russian refusenik, a US senator, a Parisian fashion designer, an American-Israeli behavioral psychologist, a world championship boxer? What brings together prime ministers and presidents, musicians and actors, Nobel prize-winners and novelists, alongside Jews of every persuasion in every corner of the globe? What lies at the heart of a global movement of thousands of volunteers and hundreds of thousands of participants across every language, culture, background, age, and place?

Shabbat.

More specifically – the passion of Jews in every corner of the globe to receive this Divine gift, and, most importantly, to share it with one another. That has been the driving energy of The Shabbat Project, the key to its unexpected story. It is profound that when God tells Moses: "I have a precious gift in My treasure house, and its name is Shabbat," His next words are: "I want to

give it to the Jewish People – go and let them know." The Talmud
learns from this a life principle – when you give someone a gift,
you must tell them about it so that they can properly appreciate
it. Shabbat is God's gift to us, and we each have a personal
calling to share it with those around us – with our family, friends,
community, with Jews all over the world. This is the vision of The
Shabbat Project. And also the vision of this book. Thank you for
taking the time to read it. And now join me in sharing this gift
with one and all.

אָמַר לוֹ הקב"ה לְמֹשֶׁה: מַתָּנָה טוֹבָה יֵשׁ לִי בְּבֵית גְּנָזַי - וְשַׁבָּת שְׁמָהּ,
וַאֲנִי מְבַקֵּשׁ לִתְּנָהּ לְיִשְׂרָאֵל - לֵךְ וְהוֹדִיעָם.

**God said to Moses, "I have a precious gift in My
treasure house, and its name is Shabbat.**

**I want to give it to the Jewish People – go and let them
know."**

– Talmud Shabbat 10b

Acknowledgements

My sincere appreciation goes to an expert team of professionals for their excellent work on this book: Simon Apfel for his outstanding editing of the manuscript and everything else I write; Rabbi Avigdor Blumenau and his learned team at Machon Meshech Chochmah, in particular Ora McCarthy for her meticulous work, Rabbi Devon Mogg, for his research assistance with the footnotes and the bibliography, and Rabbi Juan-Paul Burke for proofreading the manuscript and for his assistance with the bibliography; Sharon Horev for her magical cover and inside layout design; Rabbi Reuven Centner and the team at Creative Chinuch for typesetting the manuscript in such a clear and beautiful way; Heidi Hurwitz for her expert sub-editing; Emily Bobrow for her invaluable editing of the initial draft of the manuscript; Laurence Horwitz for helping me formulate chapter headings for the book; and Rabbi Yochanan Slater, Sarah Saghroun, and Ariana Wajswol for translating the Hebrew, French, and Spanish editions, respectively; thanks also to Naomi Dinur, Yaacov Benisty, and Sara Efrati for proofreading the Hebrew, French, and Spanish manuscripts.

With Grateful Thanks

To the South African Jewish community, whose warm embrace of The Shabbat Project when it was first introduced showed the rest of the world what was possible. We are well known for our unity and resilience and Jewish pride – and now also as a dynamic laboratory for creative ideas for the Jewish people. It is my great privilege and pleasure to serve this magnificent community.

To the thousands of Shabbat Project volunteers in cities around the world, the lifeblood of the project. You are genuine trailblazers. With ingenuity and passion, you have taken ownership of the project and made it come alive. A tiny fraction of your stories are told in this book, but God has recorded all of them for your eternal merit. And to Laurence Horwitz, Rosy Hollander, and Tanya Harati for your remarkable dedication and hard work to help me establish The Shabbat Project.

To George Walkley for overseeing the production and distribution of this book. To Robby Nissan, Sharon Horev, Marc Maley and Brett Morris for your innovation and creativity in crafting the communication strategy for the book, and to Daniel Tucker for your insights and hard work in implementing the plan, with the dedicated assistance of Tali Blumenau. To Neil Blair for your advice and assistance on publishing this book, and on much else, and, especially, for introducing me to so many remarkable people.

To the countless partners and friends who have accompanied and supported me on the journey of The Shabbat Project and this book, and much else. A special thank you to Steven Blumgart, Robbie Brozin, David Chitrin, Amit Cohen, Isy Danon, Dr. Richard Friedland, Daniel Ginsburg, Adrian Gore, Steven Herring, Larry Heyman, Rodney Ichikowitz, Steven Kalmin, David and Graeme Lazarus, Herschel Mayers, the Moritz family, Benjy Porter, Ralph Rieder, Ivan and Lynette Saltzman, the Sassoon family, and Larry Wolfe for your generosity, partnership, and friendship over the years.

To Selwyn Schaffer, who donated towards the production costs of the book in memory of his father, Yaakov Leib ben Shmuel Halevi; and to Sharon Wapnick, who did so in memory of her parents, Alec and Joan Wapnick, and grandparents, Morrie and Fay Kramer. To Rabbi Moshe Lewin and Emilio Penhos for your friendship and partnership, and for ensuring the sponsorship and distribution of the French and Spanish editions of the book, respectively.

To President Isaac Herzog for your friendship and support for The Shabbat Project, both as Chairman of the Jewish Agency, and now as Israel's President; to Senator Joe Lieberman and Natan Sharansky for your support and guidance as members of the International Advisory Board of The Shabbat Project; to Professor Dan Ariely for your advice on The Shabbat Project at its inception, and for all your insights since then on many other things.

To Gary Torgow for your support, advice, and partnership on The Shabbat Project and everything else. And of course to my dear anonymous friend in Detroit for your confidence in me and overwhelming generosity.

To Martin and Anthony Moshal, two remarkable brothers, who have been my close friends and partners for so many years, for your generosity, your vision, and your grace and humility (often thanking me for the opportunity to contribute whenever I tried to thank you).

To Jeffrey and Elana Samson, Dorothy and Leonard Sank, Franki and Steven Cohen, for taking the baton of philanthropy and leadership from your legendary father Eric Samson of blessed memory. Your relentless drive for a better world gives eloquent expression to your father's legacy.

To the UOS boards of Johannesburg and Cape Town for your support and partnership for more than 18 years. We share the vision that spreading Torah and mitzvahs is the key to a vibrant future for our community. The Shabbat Project and this book are part of realizing that vision.

To Rabbi Shmuel Kamenetsky, Torah giant of our generation, for your guidance and encouragement with the Shabbat Project from the beginning, for always being accessible for advice despite carrying all of Klal Yisrael on your shoulders, and, most recently, for your generous words of endorsement for this book. To Rabbi Osher Weiss, posek for communities around the world, for being graciously responsive in providing halachic instruction whenever needed for me and my community. To Rabbi Berel Wein, visionary leader and thinker, thank you for your sage insight and guidance, and warm encouragement, every step of the way in my journey of rabbinic service.

To my late teacher, mentor and Rosh Yeshiva, Rabbi Azriel Chaim Goldfein of blessed memory, for giving me, and his many students, the most precious gift of his teaching and wisdom. The Rosh Yeshiva's insistence on teaching Torah from the sources shaped my approach to writing this book, and his visionary leadership inspired me to create The Shabbat Project – though, to my sadness, he never lived to see either.

To my dear brothers – my best friends and full partners in everything – Colin and Saul. None of the work I've done for more than 25 years as a rabbi would have been possible without your unwavering support, love, partnership, advice, and loyalty. And to our dear parents, for your relentless selflessness, guidance, and love in raising the three of us to be dreamers who try to make the world a better place.

To my dear wife Gina, and our precious children Mordechai and Avigayil, Levi and Michal, Shayna, Azriel, and our sparkling arrival, the first of a new generation, Tzofiya, for your unconditional love, support, and encouragement, and for bringing me so much joy every day. Gina has been my partner in everything – including The Shabbat Project. From the beginning, she helped formulate its vision, and determine the direction of the project as it evolved. It was Gina who guided us to a life of service and leadership in the rabbinate, and who has stood by my side with so much strength and loyalty through it all. As Rabbi Akiva once told his students about his wife Rachel: "What's mine and yours, is hers."

And, finally, my overwhelming gratitude to the One Who gave us all the awesome gift of Shabbat, our beloved Creator Who "has given us life, sustained us, and brought us to this moment."

Index to Practical Aspects of Shabbat

This index is a companion to the table of contents, and references the places in the book that discuss the deeper meaning behind the practical aspects of Shabbat. It is important because a key message of the book is that the ideas of Shabbat cannot be separated from how they are expressed through our actions, as designed by the *halacha*. This is more than just a book of collected thoughts. It seeks to bring these ideas to life every week, as a means of integrating the philosophy of Shabbat with the immersive experience of the day.

Kiddush
Chapters 3, 6, 17, 18, 21, 29, 31, 34, 35, 42, 44

Blessing children
Chapters 6, 30

Three meals
Chapters 3, 6, 10, 24, 26, 30, 31, 34, 38

Two challahs
Chapters 8, 10

Shabbat table zemirot (songs)
Mizmor LeDavid – chapter: 8
Mah Yedidut – chapters: 24, 30, 37, 44
Yom Shabbaton – chapters: 38, 39

Enjoying Shabbat
Chapters 3, 10, 24, 34, 35

Honoring Shabbat
Chapters 3, 24, 35

Learning Torah on Shabbat
Chapters 3, 6, 7, 12, 20, 31, 35, 37

Havdalah
Chapters 3, 8, 12, 29, 42, 43

Melave malka (post-Shabbat meal)
Chapter 43

Awareness of Shabbat during the week
Chapters 14, 21, 43

Bibliography

As is clear from all the notes in the preceding pages, we have not walked this journey to discover Shabbat on our own. Every step of the way, we have been guided by the Written and Oral Torah, given by God at Sinai in 1313 B.C.E.,[1] along with the writings and teachings of the great sages of Jewish history, spanning eras and continents, drawing on their accumulated insights into these holy texts. Together, by exploring their ideas in this book, we join a

---

[1] Certain parts of the Torah were committed to writing by Moses, as dictated by God, before this date (Rashi, Exodus 24:1, Exodus 24:7, based on Midrash, Mechilta D'Rabbi Yishmael 19:10). Rabbi Yishmael holds that the general mitzvahs were given at Sinai on this date and the details were given by God over the remaining 40 years in the desert. However, Rabbi Akiva holds that the mitzvahs were given with their details at Mt. Sinai (Talmud, Chagigah 6a-b; Talmud, Sotah 37b; Talmud, Zevachim 115b). For a discussion of apparent exceptions according to Rabbi Akiva's opinion see Mizrachi, Numbers 11:10; Ohr HaChaim, Numbers 27:5; Chidushei Chatam Sofer, Niddah 49b; Chazon Ish, O.C. 125. All agree that the Torah was not committed to writing in its entirety until the end of the 40 years in the desert, on the day Moses passed away (Talmud, Taanit 30b; Talmud, Bava Batra 121b; Mechilta D'Rabbi Yishmael 12:1; Sifra, Vayikra Dibbura d'Nedavah, 2:13; see also Talmud, Gittin 60a). Once Moses had passed away, there could be no prophetic amendments to the Torah (Talmud, Shabbat 104a, Talmud, Yoma 80a and Talmud, Megillah 2b derive this from Leviticus 27:3). This is because every word contained in the Chumash is the direct word of God as dictated to Moses, whether at Sinai or during the 40 years, as per this footnote and the next, which explains the uniqueness of the Chumash in contrast to the later parts of the Written Torah.

268

grand cross-generational conversation that God began with us at Sinai. These, then, are the sources that have lit the path for us:

The Written Torah

The Written Torah comprises the Chumash, the "Five Books," which God dictated word for word to Moses; and also the later prophetic writings, the last of which were concluded by 400 B.C.E. Together, they are referred to as the Tanach,[2] and consist of 24 books, each of which have been referred to in this work.

The Oral Torah

The Oral Torah was given by God to Moses, and handed down through the generations in an unbroken line of transmission from teacher to student, all the way through to the sages of the Talmudic era (approx. 400 B.C.E. – 500 C.E), who distilled these teachings into certain key texts. Some of these texts existed as manuscripts that were only formally published in later centuries. Here is a list of the Oral Torah sources referenced in the book:

Avot D'Rabbi Natan compilation of Tannaic teachings pertaining to Pirkei Avot, compiled by Rabbi Natan the Babylonian | c.100s | Land of Israel, Roman Empire

Babylonian Talmud compilation of the Oral Torah, including the Mishna and Gemara, of the Sages of Babylonia, edited by Rav

---

[2] The word "Tanach" is an acronym for "Torah" (Chumash), "Neviim" (Prophets) and "Ketuvim" (Writings). The Chumash is the direct word of God; the books of the Neviim were written with the spirit of prophecy, known as *nevuah*, that comes directly from God; and the Ketuvim were written with a level of Divine communication just below prophecy, known as *ruach hakodesh*. (Rambam, Guide for the Perplexed 1:40, 1:45, 2:45; based on II Samuel 23:2; Radak, Introduction to Tehillim, based on Talmud, Berachot 4b).

Ashi | 352-427 | Sura, Babylonia, Sasanian Empire; and Ravina II | c.500 | Sura, Babylonia, Sasanian Empire

Jerusalem Talmud compilation of the Oral Torah, including the Mishna and Gemara, of the Sages of the Land of Israel, edited by Rabbi Yochanan bar Nafcha | 180-279 | Sepphoris/Tiberias, Land of Israel, Roman Empire

Midrash Aggada anonymous Aggadic Midrashic collection, possibly compiled in c.1000s (later edited and published by Solomon Buber | 1827-1906 | Lvov-Lemberg, Austro-Hungarian Empire)

Midrash Bamidbar Rabba Aggadic Midrash consisting of the sections of the Midrash Rabba on the book of Numbers, possibly compiled by Rabbi Oshaya | c.200 | or Rabbi Moshe HaDarshan | c.1000s

Midrash Bereishit Rabba Aggadic Midrash consisting of the sections of the Midrash Rabba on the book of Genesis compiled by Rabbi Oshaya (and added to by later Talmudic Sages) | c.200 | Caesarea, Land of Israel, Roman Empire

Midrash Devarim Rabba Aggadic Midrash consisting of the sections of the Midrash Rabba on the book of Deuteronomy compiled by the Babylonian Geonim | c.900 | Babylonia, Abbasid Caliphate

Midrash Kohelet Rabba Aggadic Midrash consisting of the sections of the Midrash Rabba on the book of Ecclesiastes compiled by the Talmudic Sages of the Land of Israel and Babylonia | c.500

Midrash Mechilta D'Rabbi Yishmael Halachic Midrash on the Book of Exodus, possibly teachings of Rabbi Yishmael ben Elisha | c.90-c.160 | Kfar Aziz, Land of Israel, Roman Empire

Midrash Pesikta D'Rav Kahana Aggadic Midrash, possibly teachings of Rav Kahana, student of Rav | c.100s | Babylonia, Parthian Empire/Sasanian Empire

Midrash Pesikta Rabbati Aggadic Midrash on the Torah, collection of the Geonic Era | c.589-c.1034 | Babylonia, Sasanian Empire/Rashidun Caliphate/Umayyad Caliphate/Abbasid Caliphate

Midrash Pirkei D'Rabbi Eliezer Aggadic Midrash consisting of the teachings of Rabbi Eliezer ben Hyrkanos | c.100s | Jerusalem/Yavne/Lod, Land of Israel, Roman Empire

Midrash Seder Olam Zutta Aggadic Midrash, anonymous work of Jewish chronology based on earlier sources and compiled by the sages of Babylonia | c.800 | Babylonia, Umayyad Caliphate/Abbasid Caliphate

Midrash Shemot Rabba Aggadic Midrash consisting of the sections of the Midrash Rabba on the book of Exodus, based, in part, on the Midrash Tanchuma | c.700 | Land of Israel, Umayyad Caliphate

Midrash Shir HaShirim Rabba Aggadic Midrash consisting of the sections of the Midrash Rabba on Song of Songs compiled by the Talmudic Sages of the Land of Israel before the compilation of the Babylonian Talmud

Midrash Sifra (Torat Kohanim) Halachic Midrash on the Book of Leviticus, compiled by Rav | c.175–c.247 | Sura, Babylonia, Parthian Empire/Sasanian Empire

Midrash Sifrei Bamidbar Halachic Midrash on the Book of Numbers, compiled by Rav | c.175–c.247 | Sura, Babylonia, Parthian Empire/Sasanian Empire

Midrash Sifrei Devarim Halachic Midrash on the Book of Deuteronomy, compiled by Rav | c.175–c.247 | Sura, Babylonia, Parthian Empire/Sasanian Empire

Midrash Tanchuma Aggadic Midrash on the Torah, including teachings of Rabbi Tanchuma bar Abba | c.360 | Land of Israel, Byzantine Empire

Midrash Tanchuma (Buber) Aggadic Midrash on the Torah, including teachings of Rabbi Tanchuma bar Abba | c.360 | Land of Israel, Byzantine Empire; edited and published by Solomon Buber | 1827-1906 | Lvov-Lemberg, Austro-Hungarian Empire

Midrash Tanna D'Vei Eliyahu (Rabba and Zutta) Aggadic Midrash, the teachings of Eliyahu HaNavi, possibly compiled by Rav Anan | c.200s | Babylonia, Parthian Empire/Sasanian Empire

Midrash Tehillim (Midrash Shocher Tov) Aggadic Midrash on the Book of Psalms possibly compiled either by Rabbi Shimon ben Rabbi Yehuda HaNasi | c.200s | Beit Shearim, Land of Israel, Roman Empire; or by Rabbi Yochanan bar Nafcha | 180-279 | Sepphoris/Tiberias, Land of Israel, Roman Empire

Midrash Vayikra Rabba Aggadic Midrash consisting of the sections of the Midrash Rabba on the book of Leviticus compiled by Rabbi Oshaya and added to by later Talmudic Sages | c.200 | Caesarea, Land of Israel, Roman Empire

Midrash Yalkut Shimoni well-known and comprehensive Midrashic anthology covering all of Tanach compiled by Rabbi Shimon HaDarshan | c.1200s | Frankfurt, Holy Roman Empire

Mishna compilation of the laws of the Oral Torah, compiled and edited by Rabbi Yehuda HaNasi (Rebbi) | c.135-c.217 | Beit Shearim/Sepphoris, Land of Israel, Roman Empire

Pesach Haggadah authorized order of the Pesach Seder and story of the Exodus from Egypt, anonymous pre-Mishnaic work by the Talmudic Sages, possibly added to later by the Amoraic Sages of Babylonia

Pirkei Avot (Mishna) Talmudic tractate on ethics, morals and character traits, edited by Rabbi Yehuda HaNasi (Rebbi) | c.135-c.217 | Beit Shearim/Sepphoris, Land of Israel, Roman Empire

Siddur the authorized prayerbook, the foundations of which were authored by the Men of the Great Assembly | c.360 BCE | Jerusalem, Land of Israel; the first known formal version was formulated by Rav Amram Gaon of Sura | c.850 | Sura, Babylonia

Targum Onkelos translation of the Torah into Aramaic by Onkelos (possibly Aquila of Sinope) | 35-120 | Land of Israel, Roman Empire

Tikkunei Zohar Kabbalistic work based on teachings of Rabbi Shimon bar Yochai | c.100s | Land of Israel, Roman Empire

Tractate Derech Eretz Zutta one of the "minor" tractates based on teachings of the Talmudic Sages not included in the Talmud, compiled by the Savoraim | c.500-c.600 | Babylonia, Sasanian Empire

Tractate Kalla Rabbati one of the "minor" tractates based on teachings of the Talmudic Sages not included in the Talmud, compiled by the Savoraim | c.500-c.600 | Babylonia, Sasanian Empire

Tractate Sofrim one of the "minor" tractates based on teachings of the Talmudic Sages not included in the Talmud, compiled by the Savoraim | c.500-c.600 | Babylonia, Sasanian Empire

Zohar Kabbalistic work based on teachings of Rabbi Shimon bar Yochai | c.100s | Land of Israel, Roman Empire

Zohar Chadash Kabbalistic work based on teachings of Rabbi Shimon bar Yochai | c.100s | Land of Israel, Roman Empire

Rabbinic Writings

From the time the Talmud was completed until the present day, our greatest rabbis have authored works explaining and interpreting the Written and Oral Torah – enabling us to appreciate the depth of these sources, understand their wide-ranging applications, and access their wisdom. Across the generations, these rabbis form a direct and unbroken line of transmission all the way back to Sinai.

Abarbanel (Nachalat Avot) Rabbi Yitzchak ben Yehuda Abarbanel | 1437-1508 | Lisbon, Kingdom of Portugal; Toledo, Kingdom of Castile

Aderet Eliyahu Rabbi Eliyahu ben Shlomo Zalman (the Vilna Gaon) | 1720-1797 | Vilna, Grand Duchy of Lithuania

Akeidat Yitzchak Rabbi Yitzchak ben Moshe Arama | c.1420-1494 | Zamora, Kingdom of Castile; Tarragona/Fraga, Kingdom of Aragon

Arizal Rabbi Yitzchak ben Shlomo Luria Ashkenazi (HaAri HaKadosh) | 1534-1572 | Tzfat, Land of Israel, Ottoman Empire

Aruch HaShulchan Rabbi Yechiel Michel Epstein | 1829-1908 | Navaredok, Russian Empire

Avnei Nezer Rabbi Shmuel Bornsztain (the Sochatchover Rebbe) | 1855-1926 | Partchev/Sochatchov, Russian Poland

Avudraham Rabbi David ben Yosef Avudraham | c.1300s | Seville, Kingdom of Castile

Bechor Shor Rabbi Yosef Bechor Shor (Rivash/Ri) | 1145-1195 | Orléans, France

Be'er HaGola Rabbi Yehuda Loew ben Betzalel (the Maharal of Prague) | 1520-1609 | Prague, Habsburg Monarchy

Beit Yitzchak Rabbi Yitzchak Yehudah Schmelkes | 1827-1905 | Lviv, Russian Empire

Beit Yosef Rabbi Yosef Karo | 1488-1575 | Tzfat, Land of Israel, Ottoman Empire

Ben Ish Chai Rabbi Yosef Chaim | 1835-1909 | Baghdad, Ottoman Empire

Biur HaGra Rabbi Eliyahu ben Shlomo Zalman (the Vilna Gaon) | 1720-1797 | Vilna, Grand Duchy of Lithuania

Bnei Yissaschar Rabbi Tzvi Elimelech Spira of Dinov | c.1783-1841 | Dinov, Habsburg Monarchy

Chidushei Chatam Sofer Rabbi Moshe Schreiber (the Chatam Sofer) | 1762–1839 | Pressburg (Bratislava), Austrian Empire

Chazon Ish Rabbi Avraham Yeshaya Karelitz (the Chazon Ish) | 1878-1953 | Kosov, Russian Empire; Vilna, Lithuania; Bnei Brak, Israel

Chidushei Aggadata Rabbi Yehuda Loew ben Betzalel (the Maharal of Prague) | 1520-1609 | Prague, Habsburg Monarchy

Chidushei Aggadot Rabbi Eliyahu ben Shlomo Zalman (the Vilna Gaon) | 1720-1797 | Vilna, Grand Duchy of Lithuania

Chizkuni Rabbi Chizkiah ben Manoach | 1250-1310 | France

Chofetz Chaim Rabbi Yisrael Meir Kagan (the Chofetz Chaim) | 1839-1933 | Radin, Russian Empire/Poland

Chofetz Chaim on the Torah Rabbi Yisrael Meir Kagan (the Chofetz Chaim) | 1839-1933 | Radin, Russian Empire/Poland

Collected Writings of Rabbi Samson Raphael Hirsch Rabbi Samson Rapahel Hirsch | 1808-1888 | Frankfurt am Main City-State/Kingdom of Prussia

Commentary on Avot (Ateret Tzvi) Rabbi Samson Raphael Hirsch | 1808-1888 | Frankfurt am Main City-State/Kingdom of Prussia

Commentary on Chumash Rabbi Samson Raphael Hirsch | 1808-1888 | Frankfurt am Main City-State/Kingdom of Prussia

Daat Torah Rabbi Yerucham Levovitz | 1873-1936 | Mir, Russian Empire/Poland

Daat Zekeinim Torah commentary compiled from the writings of the Baalei Tosafot, various authors | 1100s-1300s | France; Germany; various editors, including Shimshon ben Avraham of Sens (the Rash) | c.1150-c.1230 | Sens, France; Jerusalem/Acre, Land of Israel, Kingdom of Jerusalem

Darash Moshe from the writings of Rabbi Moshe Feinstein | 1895-1986 | Uzda, Russian Empire; Liuban, Russian Empire/ Soviet Union; Staten Island, New York, USA

Darosh Darash Yosef oral discourses of Rabbi Yosef Dov Soloveitchik | 1903-1993 | Boston, Massachusetts, USA; edited by Rabbi Avishai David | 1949-present | Jerusalem, Israel

Darchei Moshe Rabbi Moshe Isserles (the Rema) | 1530-1572 | Krakow, Kingdom of Poland

Derech Chaim Rabbi Yehuda Loew ben Betzalel (the Maharal of Prague) | 1520-1609 | Prague, Habsburg Monarchy

Derech Hashem Rabbi Moshe Chaim Luzzatto (the Ramchal) | 1707-1746 | Padua, Republic of Venice; Amsterdam, Dutch Republic; Acre, Land of Israel, Ottoman Empire

Drasha for Shabbat HaGadol Rabbi Yehuda Loew ben Betzalel (the Maharal of Prague) | 1520-1609 | Prague, Habsburg Monarchy

Ein Ayah Rabbi Avraham Yitzchak Kook | 1865-1935 | Jerusalem, Land of Israel, British Mandate of Palestine

Eitz Chaim Rabbi Chaim Vital | 1542-1620 | Tzfat, Land of Israel, Ottoman Empire; Damascus, Ottoman Empire

Emet LeYaakov Rabbi Yaakov Kamenetsky | 1891-1986 | Tzitavyan, Lithuania; New York, New York, USA

Emunah U'Vitachon Rabbi Avraham Yeshaya Karelitz (the Chazon Ish) | 1878-1953 | Kosov, Russian Empire; Vilna, Lithuania; Bnei Brak, Israel

Emunot V'Deot Rav Saadia Gaon | 882-942 | Egypt, Abbasid Caliphate; Land of Israel, Abbasid Caliphate; Sura, Babylonia, Abbasid Caliphate

Eretz Tzvi Rabbi Tzvi Hersh Bonhardt | c.1747-1810 | Kingdom of Poland

Even Sheleima collected writings of Rabbi Eliyahu ben Shlomo Zalman (the Vilna Gaon) | 1720-1797 | Vilna, Grand Duchy of Lithuania; edited with notes by Rabbi Shmuel Maltzen | 1700s | Slutsk, Russian Empire

Gevurot Hashem Rabbi Yehuda Loew ben Betzalel (the Maharal of Prague) | 1520-1609 | Prague, Habsburg Monarchy

Guide for the Perplexed Rabbi Moshe ben Maimon (the Rambam; Maimonides) | 1135-1204 | Córdoba, Almoravid Dynasty; Fustat, Ayyubid Dynasty

Gur Aryeh Rabbi Yehuda Loew ben Betzalel (the Maharal of Prague) | 1520-1609 | Prague, Habsburg Monarchy

HaKetav VeHaKabbala Rabbi Yaakov Tzvi Mecklenburg | 1785-1865 | Lisa, Kingdom of Prussia

Halachic Man Rabbi Yosef Dov Soloveitchik | 1903-1993 | Boston, Massachusetts, USA

Horeb Rabbi Samson Raphael Hirsch | 1808-1888 | Frankfurt am Main City-State/Kingdom of Prussia

Ibn Ezra Rabbi Avraham ben Meir Ibn Ezra | 1089-1167 | Tudela, Kingdom of Navarre

Iggeret HaGra Rabbi Eliyahu ben Shlomo Zalman (The Vilna Gaon) | 1720-1797 | Vilna, Grand Duchy of Lithuania

Iggeret HaRamban Rabbi Moshe ben Nachman (the Ramban; Nachmanides) | 1194-1270 | Girona, Catalonia, Kingdom of Aragon; Jerusalem/Acre, Land of Israel, Mamluk Sultanate

Iggeret of Rav Sherira Gaon (Sefer HaYuchsin) Rav Sherira Gaon | c.906-c.1006 | Pumbedita, Babylonia, Abbasid Caliphate

Iggerot Moshe Rabbi Moshe Feinstein | 1895-1986 | Uzda, Russian Empire; Liuban, Russian Empire/Soviet Union; Staten Island, New York, USA

Kad HaKemach Rabbi Bachya ben Asher ibn Halawa (Rabbeinu Bechaye) | 1255-1340 | Zaragoza, Kingdom of Aragon

Kitvei HaRamban Rabbi Moshe ben Nachman (the Ramban; Nachmanides) | 1194-1270 | Girona, Catalonia, Kingdom of Aragon; Jerusalem/Acre, Land of Israel, Mamluk Sultanate

Kitvei HaSaba MiKelm Rabbi Simcha Zissel Ziv Broide (the Alter of Kelm) | 1824-1898 | Kelm, Russian Empire

Kli Yakar Rabbi Shlomo Ephraim Luntschitz | 1550-1619 | Prague, Habsburg Monarchy

Kol Bo unknown author | c.1250-c.1450

Kuntres Hilchot Talmud Torah Rabbi Shneur Zalman of Liadi (the Baal HaTanya) | 1745-1813 | Liozna/Liadi, Grand Duchy of Lithuania/Russian Empire

Kuzari Rabbi Yehuda HaLevi | 1075-1141 | Toledo, Kingdom of Castile

Lecha Dodi (song) Rabbi Shlomo HaLevi Alkabetz | 1500-1576 | Tzfat, Land of Israel, Ottoman Empire

Likutei Sichot Rabbi Menachem Mendel Schneerson (the Lubavitcher Rebbe) | 1902-1994 | New York, New York, USA

Likutei Torah Rabbi Shneur Zalman of Liadi (the Baal HaTanya) | 1745-1813 | Liozna/Liadi, Grand Duchy of Lithuania/Russian Empire

Mah Yedidut (song) possibly composed by Rabbi Menachem ben Helbo Kara | 1015-1085 | France; or Rabbi Menachem of Le Mans | c.900s | France

Ma'avar Yabbok Rabbi Aaron Berechia of Modena | d.1639 | Modena, Italy

Machatzit HaShekel Rabbi Shmuel ben Natan Nota HaLevi Loew | c.1720-1806 | Boskovice, Moravia, Habsburg Monarchy

Machzor Vitry Rabbi Simcha ben Shmuel of Vitry | d.1105 | Vitry, France

Magen Avot Rabbi Shimon ben Tzemach Duran (the Rashbatz) | 1361-1444 | Algiers, Kingdom of Tlemcen

Magen Avraham Rabbi Avraham Gombiner | 1635-1682 | Kalish, Kingdom of Poland

Maharsha Rabbi Shmuel Eidels | 1555-1631 | Krakow/Posen, Kingdom of Poland

Malbim Rabbi Meir Leibush ben Yechiel Michel Wisser | 1809-1879 | Wreschen/Kempen, Kingdom of Prussia; Bucharest, United Principalities of Moldavia and Wallachia/Romanian United Principalities

Maor Einayim Rabbi Menachem Nachum Twersky | 1730-1787 | Chernobyl, Kingdom of Poland

Megaleh Amukot Rabbi Natan Nota Shapira | 1585-1633 | Krakow, Kingdom of Poland

Meiri Rabbi Menachem ben Shlomo Meiri | 1249-1306 | Perpignan, Principality of Catalonia/Kingdom of Majorca

Meshech Chochmah Rabbi Meir Simchah HaKohen (the Ohr Same'ach) | 1843-1926 | Butrimantz, Russian Empire; Dvinsk, Latvia

Mesilat Yesharim Rabbi Moshe Chaim Luzzatto (the Ramchal) | 1707-1746 | Padua, Republic of Venice; Amsterdam, Dutch Republic; Acre, Land of Israel, Ottoman Empire

Michtav M'Eliyahu (Strive for Truth) Rabbi Eliyahu Eliezer Dessler | 1892-1953 | London/Gateshead, England; Bnei Brak, Israel; compiled by his students: Rabbi Aryeh Carmell | 1917-2006

| London, England | Rabbi Chaim Friedlander | 1923-1986 | Bnei Brak, Israel

Midrash Lekach Tov (Pesikta Zutreta) Tobiah ben Eliezer | c.1060-c.1130 | Kastoria, Byzantine Empire

Midrash Talpiot Eliyahu ben Shlomo Avraham HaKohen | c.1650-1729 | Smyrna, Ottoman Empire

Minchat Shlomo Rabbi Shlomo Zalman Auerbach | 1910-1995 | Jerusalem, Israel

Mishna Berura Rabbi Yisrael Meir Kagan (the Chofetz Chaim) | 1839-1933 | Radin, Russian Empire/Poland

Mishne Torah Rabbi Moshe ben Maimon (the Rambam; Maimonides) | 1135-1204 | Córdoba, Almoravid Dynasty; Fustat, Ayyubid Dynasty

Mizrachi Rabbi Eliyahu ben Avraham Mizrachi | 1435-1526 | Constantinople, Ottoman Empire

Nefesh HaChaim Rabbi Chaim ben Yitzchak of Volozhin (Reb Chaim Volozhiner) | 1749-1821 | Volozhin, Russian Empire

Netivot Olam Rabbi Yehuda Loew ben Betzalel (the Maharal of Prague) | 1520-1609 | Prague, Habsburg Monarchy

Netivot Shalom Rabbi Sholom Noach Berezovsky (the Slonimer Rebbe) | 1911-2000 | Baranovitsh, Belarus; Jerusalem, Israel

Netzach Yisrael Rabbi Yehuda Loew ben Betzalel (the Maharal of Prague) | 1520-1609 | Prague, Habsburg Monarchy

Nineteen Letters, The Rabbi Samson Raphael Hirsch | 1808-1888 | Frankfurt am Main City-State/Kingdom of Prussia

Ohel Yaakov Rabbi Yaakov Krantz (the Dubno Maggid) | 1741-1804 | Dubno, Kingdom of Poland

Ohr Gedalyahu Rabbi Gedaliah Schorr | 1910-1979 | Istrik, Poland; New York, New York, USA

Ohr HaChaim Rabbi Chaim ibn Attar | 1696-1743 | Meknes, Sultanate of Morocco; Jerusalem, Land of Israel, Ottoman Empire

Ohr HaTzafun Rabbi Natan Tzvi Finkel (the Alter of Slabodka) | 1849-1927 | Rasayn, Russian Empire; Hebron, Land of Israel, British Mandate of Palestine

Olam HaYedidut Rabbi Shlomo Wolbe | 1914-2005 | Berlin, Germany; Jerusalem, Israel

On Repentance oral discourses of Rabbi Yosef Dov Soloveitchik | 1903-1993 | Boston, Massachusetts, USA; edited by Rabbi Pinchas HaKohen Peli | 1930-1989 | Jerusalem, Israel; New York, USA

Oznaim LaTorah Rabbi Zalman Sorotzkin | 1881-1966 | Zhetl, Russian Empire; Lutzk, Poland; Jerusalem, Israel

Pachad Yitzchak Rabbi Yitzchak Hutner | 1906-1980 | Warsaw, Poland; New York, New York, USA

Pirkei Moed Rabbi Mordechai Gifter | 1915-2001 | Portsmouth, Virginia/Cleveland, Ohio, USA

Pirkei Moshe Rabbi Moshe Almosnino | 1515-1580 | Istanbul, Ottoman Empire

Pirkei Torah Rabbi Mordechai Gifter | 1915-2001 | Portsmouth, Virginia/Cleveland, Ohio, USA

Pri Tzadik Rabbi Tzadok HaKohen Rabinowitz of Lublin | 1823-1900 | Lublin, Russian Poland

Raavad Rabbi Avraham ben David | 1125-1198 | Provence, France

Rabbeinu Bechaye Rabbi Bechaye ben Asher ibn Halawa | 1255-1340 | Zaragoza, Kingdom of Aragon

Rabbeinu Yona Rabbi Yona ben Avraham Girondi | 1200-1263 | Girona, Catalonia, Kingdom of Aragon

Radak Rabbi David Kimchi | 1160-1235 | Narbonne, France

Rambam, Peirush HaMishnayot Rabbi Moshe ben Maimon (the Rambam; Maimonides) | 1135-1204 | Córdoba, Almoravid Dynasty; Fustat, Ayyubid Dynasty

Ramban Rabbi Moshe ben Nachman (the Ramban; Nachmanides) | 1194-1270 | Girona, Catalonia, Kingdom of Aragon; Jerusalem/ Acre, Land of Israel, Mamluk Sultanate

Rashba Rabbi Shlomo ben Avraham ibn Aderet | 1235-1310 | Barcelona, Catalonia, Kingdom of Aragon

Rashbam Rabbi Shmuel ben Meir | c.1085-c.1158 | France

Rashi Rabbi Shlomo Yitzchaki | 1040-1105 | Troyes, France

Reflections of the Rav Rabbi Avraham R. Besdin | 1922/3-1994 | New York, New York, USA; adapted from lectures of Rabbi Yosef Dov Soloveitchik | 1903-1993 | Boston, Massachusetts, USA

Rema Rabbi Moshe Isserles | 1520-1572 | Krakow, Kingdom of Poland

Rinat Yitzchak Rabbi Yitzchak of Volozhin (Reb Itzele Volozhiner) | 1780-1849 | Volozhin, Russian Empire

Rosh Rabbi Asher ben Yechiel | 1250/1259-1327 | Cologne/ Worms, Germany; Toledo, Kingdom of Castile

Ruach Chaim Rabbi Chaim ben Yitzchak of Volozhin (Reb Chaim Volozhiner) | 1749-1821 | Volozhin, Russian Empire

Sacred and Profane (article) Rabbi Yosef Dov Soloveitchik |
1903-1993 | Boston, Massachusetts, USA

Seder HaDorot Rabbi Yechiel Heilprin | c.1660-c.1746 | Glusk/
Minsk, Kingdom of Poland

Sefer HeAruch Rabbi Natan ben Yechiel | c.1035-1110 | Rome,
Italy

Sefer HaMitzvot Rabbi Moshe ben Maimon (the Rambam;
Maimonides) | 1135-1204 | Córdoba, Almoravid Dynasty; Fustat,
Ayyubid Dynasty

Sefer HaTishbi Rabbi Elia Levita | 1469-1549 | Padua/Venice/
Rome, Italy; Isny, Germany

Sefer Chassidim Rabbi Yehuda ben Shmuel of Regensburg
(Rabbi Yehuda HeChasid) | 1150-1217 | Regensburg, Germany

Sefer HaIkkarim Rabbi Yosef Albo | c.1380-1444 | Spain

Sefer HaChaim Rabbi Chaim ben Betzalel | c.1520-1588 |
Worms/Friedberg, Germany

Sefer HaChinuch possibly Rabbi Aaron ben Yosef HaLevi (the
Ra'ah) | c.1235-c.1300 | Barcelona, Catalonia, Kingdom of Aragon

Sefer Mitzvot Gadol Rabbi Moshe ben Yaakov of Coucy (the
Semag) | 1200s | France; Spain

Sefer Mitzvot Katan Rabbi Yitzchak ben Yosef of Corbeil (the
Semak) | d.1280 | Corbeil, France

Sfat Emet Rabbi Yehuda Aryeh Leib Alter | 1847-1905 | Ger,
Russian Empire

Sforno Rabbi Ovadia Sforno | 1475-1550 | Cesena/Bologna, Italy

She'iltot Rav Achai Gaon | 680-752 | Pumbedita, Babylonia, Umayyad Caliphate

Shem MiShmuel Rabbi Shmuel Bornsztain (the Sochatchover Rebbe) | 1855-1926 | Partchev/Sochatchov, Russian Poland

Shemona Perakim Rabbi Moshe ben Maimon (the Rambam; Maimonides) | 1135-1204 | Córdoba, Almoravid Dynasty; Fustat, Ayyubid Dynasty

Shiurei Daat Rabbi Elya Meir Bloch | 1894-1954 | Telz, Lithuania; Cleveland, Ohio, USA

Shiurei Daat Rabbi Yosef Yehudah Leib Bloch | 1860-1929 | Rasayn/Telz, Russian Empire/Lithuania

Shelah (Shnei Luchot HaBrit) Rabbi Yeshayahu HaLevi Horowitz (the Shelah) | 1555-1630 | Prague, Habsburg Monarchy; Tzfat, Land of Israel, Ottoman Empire

Shulchan Aruch Rabbi Yosef Karo | 1488-1575 | Tzfat, Land of Israel, Ottoman Empire

Shulchan Aruch HaGraz Rabbi Shneur Zalman of Liadi (the Baal HaTanya) | 1745-1813 | Liozna/Liadi, Grand Duchy of Lithuania/ Russian Empire

Sichot Mussar Rabbi Chaim Shmuelevitz | 1902-1979 | Kovno, Lithuania; Jerusalem, Israel

Siddur Beit Yaakov (Siddur of Rabbi Yaakov Emden) Rabbi Yaakov Emden (the Yaavetz) | 1697-1776 | Altona, Kingdom of Denmark; Emden, Germany

Siddur HaGra Rabbi Eliyahu ben Shlomo Zalman (the Vilna Gaon) | 1720-1797 | Vilna, Grand Duchy of Lithuania

Siddur HaGra, Imrei Shefer (commentary on Siddur HaGra)
Rabbi Naftali Hertz Widenbaum | 1852-1902 | Jaffa, Land of Israel,
Ottoman Empire

Siddur of Rabbi Yichye Salach Rabbi Yichye Salach (the
Maharitz) | 1713-1805 | Sana'a, Ottoman Empire

Sifrei Chofetz Chaim: *Shem Olam* Rabbi Yisrael Meir Kagan
(the Chofetz Chaim) | 1839-1933 | Radin, Russian Empire/Poland

Taamei HaMinhagim Rabbi Avraham Yitzchak Sperling |
c.1851-c.1921 | Lvov-Lemberg, Austro-Hungarian Empire

Tanya Rabbi Shneur Zalman of Liadi (the Baal HaTanya) | 1745-
1813 | Liozna/Liadi, Grand Duchy of Lithuania/Russian Empire

Taz (Turei Zahav) Rabbi David HaLevi Segal | c.1586-1667 |
Ostrog/Lvov-Lemberg, Kingdom of Poland

Teshuvot HaRosh Rabbi Asher ben Yechiel (Rosh) | 1250/1259-
1327 | Cologne/Worms, Germany; Toledo, Kingdom of Castile

Tiferet Yisrael Rabbi Yehuda Loew ben Betzalel (the Maharal of
Prague) | 1520-1609 | Prague, Habsburg Monarchy

Tiferet Yisrael Rabbi Yisrael Lipschitz | 1782-1860 | Danzig,
Kingdom of Prussia

Tomer Devora Rabbi Moshe Cordovero (the Ramak) | 1522-1570
| Tzfat, Land of Israel, Ottoman Empire

Torah Ohr Rabbi Shneur Zalman of Liadi (the Baal HaTanya)
| 1745-1813 | Liozna/Liadi, Grand Duchy of Lithuania/Russian
Empire

Torat Avraham Rabbi Avraham Grodzinski | 1883-1944 | Kovno,
Lithuania

Torat HaAdam Rabbi Moshe ben Nachman (the Ramban; Nachmanides) | 1194-1270 | Girona, Catalonia, Kingdom of Aragon; Jerusalem/Acre, Land of Israel, Mamluk Sultanate

Tosafot various authors | 1100s-1300s | France; Germany; various editors, including Shimshon ben Avraham of Sens (the Rash) | c.1150-c.1230 | Sens, France; Jerusalem/Acre, Land of Israel, Kingdom of Jerusalem

Tur (Arba'a Turim) Rabbi Yaakov ben Asher | 1269-1343 | Toledo, Kingdom of Castile

Tzeida LaDarech Rabbi Menachem ben Aaron ibn Zerach | d.1385 | Alcala/Toledo, Kingdom of Castile

Yaarot Devash Rabbi Yonatan Eybeschutz | 1690-1764 | Prague, Habsburg Monarchy; Hamburg City-State

Yaavetz Rabbi Yosef Yaavetz | 1440-1508 | Spain; Mantua, Italy

Yom Shabbaton (song) possibly composed by Rabbi Yehuda HaLevi | 1075-1141 | Toledo, Kingdom of Castile